Joyful Teaching

Joyful Teaching

Being the Teacher You Admired

Barry Raebeck

ROWMAN & LITTLEFIELD
Lanham • Boulder • New York • London

Published by Rowman & Littlefield
An imprint of The Rowman & Littlefield Publishing Group, Inc.
4501 Forbes Boulevard, Suite 200, Lanham, Maryland 20706
www.rowman.com

86-90 Paul Street, London EC2A 4NE

Copyright © 2023 by Barry Raebeck

All rights reserved. No part of this book may be reproduced in any form or by any electronic or mechanical means, including information storage and retrieval systems, without written permission from the publisher, except by a reviewer who may quote passages in a review.

British Library Cataloguing in Publication Information Available

Library of Congress Cataloging-in-Publication Data

Names: Raebeck, Barry, author.
Title: Joyful teaching: being the teacher you admired / Barry Raebeck.
Description: Lanham, Maryland: Rowman & Littlefield, [2023] | Includes bibliographical references and index.
Identifiers: LCCN 2022054694 (print) | LCCN 2022054695 (ebook) | ISBN 9781475867596 (Cloth) | ISBN 9781475867602 (Paperback) | ISBN 9781475867619 (eBook)
Subjects: LCSH: Effective teaching—United States. | School improvement programs—United States. | Educational change—United States. | Learning.
Classification: LCC LB1025.3 .R34 2023 (print) | LCC LB1025.3 (ebook) | DDC 371.102—dc23/eng/20221206
LC record available at https://lccn.loc.gov/2022054694
LC ebook record available at https://lccn.loc.gov/2022054695

*To Mr. Philip Wachtel,
a most admirable teacher, coach, and human being*

Contents

Foreword		ix
	Chloe Hase	
Preface: Joy and Rigor: Hilarity and Expectations		xi
Acknowledgments		xvii
1	What Are We Doing Today?	1
2	Why Are We Doing This?	11
3	Teaching to Your Students	17
4	They Will Care for You When You Care for Them	25
5	Sit Down and Shut Up: Secrets of Classroom Management	31
6	The Classroom as a Home	39
7	The Classroom as a Theater	43
8	Highly Effective Assessment	49
9	More Terrific Assignments	61
10	Making and Keeping Parents Happy	73
11	Building Relationships	77
12	Coda: Joyful Teaching	83

Appendix	87
Bibliography	93
Index	95
About the Author	99

Foreword

It has been nearly a decade since I sat in Dr. Raebeck's English classroom as a fifteen-year-old. Like my peers, I had just begun the everlasting journey toward self-discovery. I have since graduated from college and have started pursuing an MA in marriage and family therapy with a specialization in trauma studies. Concurrently, I work as a residential counselor for adolescents struggling with suicidal ideation. My facility provides comprehensive dialectical behavioral therapy and centralizes the core dialectic of change and acceptance. How do we motivate an adolescent toward growth while validating their current state? How do we offer unconditional positive regard and radical genuineness? How do we hold limits and extend grace? How can we incorporate play and joy in the midst of pain and transition? These are some questions that have guided my work with youth in Los Angeles. Little did I know, answers to these questions were modeled to me in my 9th grade English classroom.

Dr. Raebeck's teaching style was dialectical in nature. He held high standards and expected effort and presence from his students. Simultaneously, he used humor, lightheartedness, and a sprinkle of absurdity to build rapport and obtain commitment from his students. Dr. Raebeck was in tune with the emotional and energetic needs of his class. There were days when reading Shakespeare was substituted with *Abbey Road* listening parties. Lesson plans were flexed to incorporate class-wide chess tournaments or full-costume reenactments of *The Importance of Being Earnest*. I looked forward to the spontaneity of English class and felt internally motivated to try my best and extend my effort.

Our class readings and discussions inspired critical thinking. I developed deep empathy for the complex and internally tormented characters introduced in beloved books. I escaped into the world of *Atonement* by Ian McEwan and felt the depth of Briony's yearning, heartache, and desire to feel seen. When reading "Hills Like White Elephants" by Ernest Hemingway, I was able to feel the weight of a woman's decision to have an abortion and considered the covert marionette strings that complicate, control, and constrict this freedom of choice.

Free periods were spent in Dr. Raebeck's classroom. Floods of students filed in daily to read, connect, edit papers, or play chess. I learned to distill the core purpose of my writing by removing the excess. I learned the importance of "controlling the center of the board" and practiced my closing strategies with patient opponents. I learned how powerful a belly laugh can be after a taxing day. I remember interviewing Dr. Raebeck for a school newspaper article in an effort to recruit new members to the chess club. Our interview, entitled "Between Two Pawns," was a cheeky rendition of comedian Zach Galifianakis's talk show *Between Two Ferns*.

Classes were energetic and tranquil, serious and humorous, spontaneous and reliable, challenging and safe. I became more confident in my voice and my writing grew stronger. I began recognizing the worth of my participation and became more willing to contribute my perspectives. As I continue to support adolescents in creating a life worth living, I look back on these formative educational experiences and accept the torch.

Chloe Hase
MFT Trauma Specialization student
Pacific Oaks College

Preface

Joy and Rigor: Hilarity and Expectations

At some point near the beginning of one's career we may come to understand that there is often a false dichotomy in effect in schools. There are tough, demanding, intelligent, unyielding teachers who espouse the need for rigor in the classroom, in the curriculum, in the school fabric, even in the wider society. Generally, these teachers are respected and valued by parents and administrators, and even by students—though often after the fact.

Then there are playful, lighthearted, gentle, and understanding souls, and they offer fun, and even joy upon occasion, but do not seem overly concerned with standards of learning or behavior. Students generally like them, and sometimes adore them. And parents and administrators like them too, though perhaps with reservations. Are they really that bright or knowledgeable? Are the kids learning enough in their classes? (And some of the most able students have those questions too.)

The tough demanding teachers don't want to waste time with what they see as frivolity. They will hold classes on weekends if allowed to do so. The only homework assignments that matter are theirs. Educating their students is a battle they intend to win at any cost. The loose, cuddly teachers are just the opposite. They don't want to push too hard or make things competitive or intense. They don't mind assemblies, locker clean-outs, or snow delays. There isn't much homework. And they love fire drills! The resultant scenario is a classic *either/or* dichotomy.

But joy and rigor are not opposing and irreconcilable forces. This is a *both/and* scenario. There is a need for balance, and the best teaching/learning experiences exude just that: they are both rigorous *and* joyful—they relate to *both* the cognitive *and* the affective domains within us. As we grow more experienced and more capable, we become more skilled at creating a classroom dynamic that is a beautiful blend of purpose and pleasure, of work and play, of pushing and easing, of calm and combustion, of seriousness and foolishness, and of rigorous intellectual endeavor and absolute mayhem. Not many English teachers go from analyzing a Shakespearean sonnet to hitting a clementine out of the window with a golden golf club. Yet that can be marvelously effective.

Reaching this conclusion that balance is essential and that students need both focus and frivolity to learn optimally may happen over time. And it is buttressed by my studies at the doctoral level and writing a dissertation that posed the question of what a truly effective modern public high school would look like if we incorporated (1) the best of learning theory and brain-based education, (2) in-depth studies of secondary schools at the time, and (3) enduring educational philosophy.

That 240-page document, written in residence at the University of Virginia Curry School of Education and entitled *A Democratic High School Classroom Process Model*, was both a rigorous exercise and grand joy to create. For its creation enabled me to steep myself in lots of extraordinary thinking by dozens of extraordinary thinkers: Locke and Voltaire, Ralph Waldo Emerson and Horace Mann, Jean Piaget and Abraham Maslow, Jerome Bruner and Maria Montessori, Joseph Chilton Pearce and John Dewey, Marshall McLuhan and Luis Alberto Machado among them, as well as Mortimer Adler, Ted Sizer, John Goodlad, and Ernest Boyer, authors of the four exceptional studies of high school in the 1980s. (Note the stark gender and racial imbalance in the sources thirty-five years ago.)

In studying those great educational theorists and philosophers I clarified my own philosophy of teaching and learning—coming to recognize that these two words cannot exist independently in schools. *Teaching/learning* is what happens. If we "teach" something, but our students do not learn it, we cannot claim otherwise. "Covering content" is not teaching/learning. We all know that, and yet that is all the more reason for teachers to develop a flexible yet thoughtful and practical philosophy to guide us.

I believe in *connections* with students, both intellectual and emotional. The cognitive and the affective are connected after all. *Each and every student is distinct and worthy*. No one can begin to claim to know what another is capable of, and no adult need to predict what an adolescent will become. Are you the same now as you were at age fifteen? Life is developmental. If you take no other saying from this book, take this one: *life is developmental.*

Parents and teachers worry *way* too much about what *could* happen. But worrying is essentially a waste of energy because what we worry about usually doesn't happen, and what we should worry about we rarely see coming. Yes? Worry and care are not synonymous of course, though often equated in the case of children. Thomas Pynchon says, "Keep cool, but care." That's another excellent aphorism, though not easy to do.

We've already discussed balance, specifically when it comes to joy and rigor. Standards and expectations should be high. I often quote Thoreau to my students: "We hit what we aim at, therefore aim high." Hold high expectations, yet in an atmosphere of encouragement, empathy, and support. (More about this when we discuss assessment and grouping in detail.)

Purposefulness is a fine motivator. The teacher must articulate "why" we are doing this, and in a manner that students come to appreciate. I continually remind students of the value of what we are doing. If I can't see fundamental value in the task before us, then it is likely students won't either. Knowledge is power. Mastery of one's language gives us opportunities and insight. Being an active listener is a wonderful skill. Having an opinion is one thing, but having an informed opinion based on research and experience is actually valuable.

Respect is another aspect of a highly functional classroom. We must expect it from students, and we must offer it as well. As informal as I can be, there are lines that I won't let students cross. "I am your friend; I am not your peer." It's also true of parenting. At the same time, I give students the benefit of the doubt when it comes to a missing assignment or a tardy or a foolish impulse. Although I have a bottom line, I believe in second and third chances. Again, these are kids—and we all make mistakes.

The important thing is to help them learn from their mistakes. The best way to ensure that happens is not always clear, especially in the moment. It is helpful to keep in mind that although we are the ultimate power in the classroom, we are also fallible, emotional, and inconsistent at times.

Case study: cheating. I don't like apps such as Turnitin, which assume that all students need to be monitored for plagiarism. I like the idea of an honor system. But these days it certainly is easy to access and submit someone else's essay or story for your English assignment. Yet, after reading literally thousands and thousands of high school papers, I got to a point where I could effectually tell the kids, "I am a human Turnitin. I will catch you. Don't plagiarize. It is a crime against humanity. You will burn in hell."

Of course, you know how this story goes—the little buggers still cheat. (Again, remember when you were sixteen or seventeen? Ever get into the old man's hooch? "Borrow" your mom's car?) Surely some get away with it, but every year pretty much once or twice I will be reading a stack of papers and get to one that just cannot be authentic. The title of this "original" short story is "Days of a Spent Man's Ignominy" or "A Trek Through the Towering Himalayas in Search of El Dorado." You might at least change the title, bozo. Yeesh.

And I get a sinking feeling in my stomach knowing that I have to deal with this mess. What if it is a student in the honor society? Cheating means expulsion from that august body. What if it is a student who normally works hard and produces good work, but took a dreadful shortcut late Sunday night? Or what if it is a kid who is tired of getting mediocre grades, tired of his parents' dissatisfaction, tired of feeling unworthy?

I don't always do the same thing, that's for sure. Yes, I feel that serious transgressions should have consequences. But I also feel that consequences should be circumstantial and flexible. Hard and inviolable "rules" that don't allow for the use of psychology or wisdom often don't serve us well. The point is not simply to punish the behavior but to change it.

I first write "SMAC" on the paper: See Me After Class. That will get the needed attention, though certain miscreants might try to escape me for a day or so. (I tell my classes, "I'm like the Royal Canadian Mounted Police. Their slogan is, 'I always get my man.'") Once the culprit is cornered, we have a one-sided conversation, short and painful. I ask if the paper is plagiarized, and get a quick confession, or a forced one. I state my disappointment. Then I list the actions that I can take, pursuant to the school policy, which include a zero, a rewrite, and notification of guidance, administration, and parents.

At this point I have the full attention of a sad and wounded little bird. At this point I already have tremendous impact. Although they may offer a few excuses, rarely, if ever, do kids insist that they have not erred, not done a bad thing. And I then say that I am not sure how I will proceed but will speak to the student the next day, a full twenty-four hours in the tortured future. (With some kids I worry more about that knowing how emotional and intense adolescents can be when in a pickle.) That tremulous waiting period is often the most effective consequence, however.

The next day I ask the student to redo the paper within a few days, saying that there will be a zero recorded for the plagiarized one. Depending somewhat on the student's demeanor, that might be the end of it. There are times when I take it to another level, but more often than not I let the experience be the lesson, imploring the student to learn from it. I don't refer it to anyone else, and I don't contact the parents. That leads to blessed relief on the part of the perp.

Finally, I remind the entire class of the severity of such a breach of our contract. I also note that if they are caught plagiarizing in college, they very well may be sent home. The reprobate will slink lower and lower in his (usually) or her (occasionally) desk, though I never mention the student in question. Perhaps someone learns a valuable lesson. Remember the bishop's candlesticks in *Les Misérables*.

Finally, when it comes to my philosophy, I believe in creating a class that I myself would wish to attend when I was fifteen, sixteen, or seventeen. If I had a choice, would I take this class, would I go to Raebeck's room third period every day? That's a powerful construct. It's quite something to take that on as a routine responsibility. When we do it well, attendance is much better, by the way. Kids rarely cut classes they look forward to, eh?

Beyond the theory and the practice, the strategies and techniques, there may be a guiding vision. Why are we doing this after all? What is the purpose of spending one's working days in a classroom with needy, squirming, aspiring, and perspiring adolescents? Teachers are routinely overworked and underpaid, overburdened, and underappreciated by the world beyond the schoolhouse doors. Teaching has the highest burn-out rate of any profession in the United States, with fully 44 percent saying they are very often or always feeling burned out at work. And this occurs far more frequently with young teachers (Bouchrika 2022).

Yet effective teachers retain a level of gratification rare in other professions. It is incumbent upon us to offer means for more teachers to thrive. Good teachers are blessing the children in their care, and so are they blessed.

I didn't choose teaching, teaching chose me. I always felt that I could be successful in a host of professions. Then I did my student teaching in the final semester as an undergraduate. In a matter of days struggling to figure out what to do before and during each class—and then feeling the resultant surge of responsive energy from my students—I was hooked. It was fun!

I knew that I wanted to share important uplifting experiences. I knew that I cared about making those young people better at the four language arts but also at life itself. I thrilled at sharing challenging perspectives and widening perceptions, sensibilities, and tolerance for new and unexpected things. Let's welcome diversity of person and thought, while building standards of decency and care. Let's become stronger thinkers, clearer writers, kinder friends, and nobler citizens. Let's give individual effort and also work together to better our world.

Having a philosophy of education to guide us is not some abstract, vapid exercise devoid from "reality." Having principles, guideposts, mentors, aspirations, ideals, slogans, and inspirations only make the endlessly challenging task of being a secondary school teacher easier. Don't push those things skeptically aside. Find some credos to teach by. Find some mantras to sing you to sleep. Rest blissfully in the knowledge that ours is a splendid calling.

Acknowledgments

So many wonderful people have made my teaching experience extraordinarily rich. I would love to acknowledge everyone who has been a part of the journey. For the sake of the reader, I must limit my kudos. And I apologize to the many deserving folks whom I have omitted.

Students are at the center of a joyful teaching experience. I say, "Thank you!" to each and every one of the approximately two thousand Southampton High School students I have had the pleasure of teaching—and learning from. I routinely said in front of a class that "I don't have a favorite student, but if I did it would be so and so!" That always brought a laugh from the group and a surprised grin from the noted individual, generally someone I knew to be unused to acclaim.

I wish to thank the parents and guardians of all these amazing young people too. It is a great responsibility to be entrusted with the education of someone's child. Thank you for that trust. And thank you for all the holiday and end-of-year presents!

Chloe Hase, whom I taught in two courses at Southampton High School and honored me by writing the foreword to this book, was a model of excellence as a scholar, and more importantly, remains so as a human being.

Mr. (Philip) Wachtel was my 8th grade English teacher, and basketball coach, at Connetquot Junior High School in Bohemia, New York. He was engaging, kind, challenging, a tremendous role model, and a consummate educator.

I had such terrific colleagues at Southampton for many years and continue to call them friends. It was a special privilege and joy to work and play alongside teachers Sean Brand, Suzana Blanco, Greg and Maria Metzger, Diane

Guida, Heather Haux, Peter Liubenov, Tim Schreck, Frank McDermott, Maria Clinton, Tippi Amares, Juni Wingfield, Sara Smith, Brian Tenety, Mitti Abbadessa, Tonya Hodges, Matt Obert, Sarah McGuire, Sherri Smith, Perri Nation, Bob Barker, Virginia McGovern, Vinnie Zangrillo, Gail Altomare, Sean Zay, and Lou Stellato among many others.

Several SHS staff who always made things better were Susan Wright, Erin Frankenbach, Amy Davis, Jim Elflein, Otis Reddick, Charlie Smith, Jerry Walker, Rosie Casacelli, and Jack Krejchi. I also greatly appreciate the support, respect, and affection received from the principal during my last ten years, Brian Zahn.

As for the most important force in my life, my family, it remains a source of encouragement, humor, joy, and most of all love. I am proud that my extraordinary daughters are all thriving in helping professions. Tessa, Emily, and Annabel continue to inspire me with their idealism, intelligence, and creative energies.

And of course, I must thank my fantastic wife, Susan, an accomplished educator and legendary kindergarten teacher in Sag Harbor for twenty-three years. She sets a high standard indeed.

Chapter 1

What Are We Doing Today?

The academic aspect of high school is a huge tub of meaningless stuff to most of the students. Now that may sound harsh to the district curriculum director, but we all know it is empirically true. Remember what you thought and felt when you were in high school. It is highly unlikely that you leapt out of bed on Monday morning in February determined to get there as early as possible, to learn as much as possible, and to "drink as much Kool Aid" as possible each day.

Even the low percentage of students who apparently thrive, the high honor roll grinders who shuck and jive and earn extra points, and the bright and talented ones with the cleanest faces and the tightest smiles rarely see much intrinsic value in what they are asked to do each day. They are the trained seals best at leaping for the thrown fish. And they are wonderful in many ways—without them the whole edifice would likely collapse. They are mature and diligent and motivated and going places. But don't believe that they are loving this.

That being said, when students enter the class and ask, "What are we doing today?" they have a certain expectation. Because most days what "we are doing" must hold some value for them, at least a little. Yes, one can argue that "only boring people are bored." At the same time, the *last* thing we want in the classroom is even a chance at boredom of any kind. Boredom is the enemy. If you find the material, the text, and the process boring, then your students will find it infinitely more so. Not only do we want every day to be different, but even teaching the same lesson to another class that day should be at least somewhat different. A dull routine is not something adolescents particularly love. Even gerbils need something different every now and then.

Plus, we have been teaching for the better part of three or twenty or thirty years. How can that not get boring, how can we not get jaded? Think of the teacher who says, "I have thirty years of teaching experience!" But actually, they may have one year of teaching experience repeated thirty times.

In twenty-two years it is possible to teach eighteen different courses, every level of student and every grade 9–12, develop and teach seven new electives in film (semester long), drama (I and II), creative writing (semester and yearlong), public speaking (semester), and college writing and preparation (semester). It is possible over the years to teach more than thirty different novels, dozens of stories, a hundred essays and articles, dozens and dozens of films, hundreds of songs and poems, and on and on.

Make certain those six five-foot-tall file cabinets are filled with materials that you know have already been of value, yet constantly come in with new stuff. (Be a bit obsessive, maybe even disturbed.) In your final year in AP Literature teach a three-week unit on Bob Dylan for the first time, using twenty of his songs, as well as video, commentary, documentary footage, and so on.

As we know, teaching a weeks-long unit of anything for the first time takes a lot of preparation. And you may never get a chance to teach it a second time—when we know that it is never the first, but often the second, and more likely at least the third time we explore a unit of study, that it all comes together. But it can still be a terrific unit—and the kids will let you know. At the end have them write the lyrics for a Dylan-esque song. The results will be fantastic. One wunderkind may even sing hers while playing guitar.

The key is *engagement*. Educators talk of engagement because it is the magic elixir. But how do we make it happen? Variety is essential, as is student direction. Giving students choices and options and open-ended assignments really works.

The "illusion of choice" is a powerful strategy with students. The illusion of choice is simply having a teacher assignment that allows for student input, perspective, and varied approaches to completing it.

This is illustrated by a wonderful assignment, *The Book Non-Report*. Students are asked to read a classic novel, after class discussion of what makes a work a classic. They have approximately three weeks, with most of the reading done outside of class and an occasional in-class reading day. Reading in class is an excellent use of class time, especially if the teacher reads too, modeling the behavior.

At the end of the novel reading, they are asked to produce a project demonstrating knowledge of several literary elements and devices in their chosen novel. Projects can be anything from dioramas to newscasts, to recitations and play-acting characters, to poetry, cartoons, book covers, diaries, acrylic paintings, interviews, student-made videos, storyboards, and so on. It's a wonderful way to provide students with alternate means of demonstrating interest and mastery of material through a skill of their choosing.

Suggest twelve or so possibilities and allow them to propose something else if that isn't on the list. Stack in a messy pile in the back of the classroom excellent projects by former students and these serve as exemplars. Before the assignment is due, bring several of the finest ones you have ever gotten and display them on the side shelves, desks, or folding tables brought in for this purpose. Exemplars are a great way to raise standards and student productivity. The more we use them over time the better results obtained.

So, assign a classic novel, but it can be from a long list, a list that is updated periodically. Reserve the right to approve the student's novel choice (on the list or gotten elsewhere) and most likely approve it so that they will be reading something they believe could be of interest. However, insist that the work be challenging and meaningful. Remind them that "it takes a great mind to write a great book. And it also takes a great mind to *read* a great book." (*The Old Man and the Sea* may be considered a classic by some, but for a project of this type it will be far too short and simple for many of your students.)

On the day projects are due, have the folding tables at the front of the room to place them on. Using a rubric that allows you to grade all of them within a few days (see chapter 9), select the better projects and display them on the tables. Invite the students to "go through the museum," seeing the work of their class and any other class that has the same assignment at that time. The best projects are admired and the students responsible are justly praised. All the kids see what a "good" project is. And the weaker projects are discreetly returned with little attention so that kids are not needlessly embarrassed. (More on student behavior and teacher expectations later.)

At the same time, it is clear that *all* of the best projects require a *lot* of effort. Far better to offer high standards, variety, student-directed learning, and opportunities for kids to do something they often find value in—rather than throw together one more "book report."

PROTECT YOUR TURF

An essential element of focus and connection is insulation from interruptions. High school is in many ways *a sustained interruption*: constant changing of classes, buzzing bells, PA announcements, kids coming in late, lockdown drills, the wall phone going off at the worst possible time (any time!), twenty-five antsy teenagers distracted by definition, cars in the driveway (including police cars, which is when certain teachers instinctively duck and cover), fire drills, assemblies, guidance presentations, visitors, loud conversations in the hallway, needless frivolity in the next room, and you have the idea.

So, Mick Jagger asks, "What can a poor boy do?" Rage against the machine. Insist that teaching time is paramount. Hold your ground. And be proactive: you may have to disconnect the electric line to the PA in your room early on. And each time they reconnect it disconnect it again (sometimes with scissors), until you wear them out. The PA in the classroom was so damned loud that we could hear an announcement anyway from the nearest hall speaker, even with the door closed. (Including lockdowns, which must be taken seriously.) And the normal announcement, whatever it was, was just a disruption—it *never* made that class better. Yes, and cut the phone lines so many times you come to think of yourself as a French partisan in WWII. And if that also kills the clock, you may have to buy a battery-operated one yourself.

In our school the single greatest enemy of class focus was the attendance officer we will call "Mrs. Martinet." She really was the reason the phone had to be disabled. That stern and well-dressed sexagenarian seemingly exalted in calling constantly, preferably in the midst of a best recitation of Shakespeare's "Sonnet 18."

In the end she was reduced to walking all the way to our door from her command post two corridors to the southwest and interrupting us that way. Or she would send a proxy, likely a rightfully fearful security monitor—usually to say that (with a minute and a half left in class) Lauren Heppenheimer's mother was waiting to take her to her orthodontist appointment. Now aren't there some others in the world who feel that Lauren would have been safe and well not knowing this for ninety seconds or that her mother could spend ninety more seconds on her phone prior to the rendezvous with her lovely child? Martinet would *not* concur, and she made the rules in that place.

Over the years, most people in the school were forced to accept that Dr. Raebeck did *not* like interruptions. Because of this, and the evisceration of so many electric wires, our classes were subject to fewer interruptions than most. And the kids came to see that it was about really wanting to be with them uninterrupted because we had so many important things to do. Teachable moments *usually* do not occur amidst cacophony and chaos. It is in the moments of calm and purposeful focus, or wild hilarity risen from common delight, that the joy of learning expands.

TECHNOLOGY

So, what are we doing today? Let's talk about multimedia and the influence of technology. When one walks the halls of a school these days it is likely that in many of the classrooms students will be staring at a screen—either the ubiquitous SMART Board or their laptop (not to mention the hideous cellphones permitted unnecessarily). In many schools the single major difference between the teaching/learning experience today and that of fifty years ago is the use of technology. Clearly that has brought benefits. Word processing is better than scratching with chalk on a slate, sharing current information quickly and accurately is better than passing a sole source reference book around the classroom, having up-to-date maps to see is better than not, and so on. There are at least two problems, though, with the modern educational embrace of technology.

The first is that as Emerson said in *Self-Reliance* in 1841, "Society never advances. It recedes as fast on one side as it gains on the other. For everything that is given, something is taken. Society acquires new arts, and loses old instincts" (Whelan 1991). It is foolish to think of human progress as some sort of unbroken line, even while it is tempting to become enamored of the latest gadget and gimmick. Offering a hard copy to students, and then reading *Self-Reliance* aloud proves far more powerful than them reading it silently on their iPads. An effective teacher telling a personal story with energy and delight remains singularly compelling. Your students will likely prefer that if given the option.

This brings us to our second problem. For years now we have reports and studies calling for young people to spend *less* time on their devices (National University 2021). And we have yet to find a reputable report or study calling for young people to spend *more* time on their devices. Parents constantly complain that their adolescents are online too much. Having them spend much of their school day online is hardly the solution. The technology director in your school or district should not be making philosophical decisions, but rather supporting the philosophical direction determined by the best educational thinking available. That is often not the case, though, is it?

Too often we see *technology for the sake of technology*. We are asked to incorporate the latest method, app, or crap, with little thought to how it is better than the predecessor—or better than nothing, for that matter. Teachers are embedded in technology in US schools now, and it is hard to see that this is leading to many great improvements.

As for the wicked cell phone, yikes! We watch in disgust as spineless administrators refuse to simply get those horrid things out of the school. They are a constant drain, and the social media addiction of teenagers has long been tied to anxiety and depression (Jacobson 2022). Kids sit in the cafeteria or study hall and don't even talk to each other. Isolated kids become more so, and all of them have shorter attention spans and less interest in things of meaning. Those enlightened secondary schools that have banned cell phone use by students during the school day, not simply in class, are to be commended. Although kids may complain, parents and teachers tend to love it.

There was constant war over cell phones because our administrators said kids should not use them during class but allowed them to use them everywhere else and keep them all day. As many colleagues didn't want to fight the daily battle, kids were often on their phones in other classes, without penalty. That made it even more difficult for those who refused to cave. The concerned teacher must confiscate them constantly and deal with the look of unconstrained horror a kid has when they are losing their phone, even for one class period.

Other suggestions include tossing them out the window (even in a rainstorm), putting them in the microwave and threatening to fry them, and routinely dumping them in the trash basket. Watching an adolescent male in the back row with his eyes down and his hands fiddling with something in his lap concealed by his desk connotes something unfathomably base. Best to eliminate that entirely. Get rid of cell phones in schools!

Case in point with the technology "improvement." When first teaching a film appreciation elective, there was no SMART Board in the class. A bulky black ROVR projection machine was obtained, a machine which would play a DVD, with excellent sound, and the capacity to show the video on a pull-down screen approximately 6' × 6'. It was a nice set-up for seeing a movie in a classroom. Then the SMART Board was installed, despite our never asking for one.

From that point on kids and staff would quite logically ask why we didn't just use the SMART Board for the films. Yes, it would have been easier, assuming we could access the desired film online for free (a large assumption). And the sound was probably just as good. But the video was NOT as good, and the screen was 4' × 5'. That's 20 square feet of movie versus 36 square feet, about one half as much. We liked the big screen. And we had the film in hand, so we weren't at the mercy of technical difficulties that invariably occur at some point with downloading. We didn't need an improvement which wasn't.

Ahh, the SMART Board (SB). Truly a mixed blessing for things other than feature films. And in time the SB was used for all manner of teaching/learning. Is it better than an old-fashioned blackboard much of the time? No. Is it nice to pull up a reference page of text and photos when starting the study of a new writer? Yes. And is it money to be able to crank out some wonderful music video on a rainy Friday morning at 7:46 AM? Ahh, indeed that is a blessing of a divine order. It is not the best thing, only the latest. And when we want to use it and it doesn't cooperate, then it is the worst thing. One day it will sit on that wall as forlornly as the oversized TV does, still on the corner mount, used only as another surface to post announcements or just silly sayings.

So, what are we doing today? As much as one may love teaching and know to offer a dynamic classroom experience, we also know that a truly functioning classroom involves everyone and multiple roles.

One of the most effective strategies for creating this is the Chapter Master activity. In the midst of a novel unit, have students pair up (by their choice generally) and present a portion of a chapter themselves. Provide them with a template of an effective Chapter Master lesson. It should include guiding questions, a passage from the text (which the students will read aloud), and unpacking the passage by denoting literary elements and devices (LEDs) therein. That last is written down to be handed in and also read to the class during the presentation. Add two follow-up questions designed to be open-ended—divergent rather than convergent. In other words, questions that do not have simple, or only one, answer to. And all the teacher does is assign students a chapter from which to draw the passage and create the related lesson. Thus, the illusion of choice again.

There is a rubric as well as a template (more on rubrics in Chapter 9). And teacher and class critique the first pair or two so that students gain a stronger understanding of what constitutes an effective presentation. They are assessed based on (1) the quality of the passage and analysis, (2) their written work, (3) their reading aloud, and (4) the relevance of their lesson in relation to the novel as a whole, as well as on our larger understanding of literature and human motivation. During these presentations, which take many days for a class of twenty to thirty kids, the teacher mainly organizes, observes, and assesses. You may ask a follow-up question to extend the thinking of the pair or the class as a whole.

It is important to provide a graded rubric for them hopefully within a day or two, assessing the oral aspects immediately and the written paper shortly thereafter. We know that the sooner feedback occurs the more value it holds. With an assignment such as a memorized Shakespearean sonnet, one is able to provide the graded rubric as soon as the student finishes the recitation and describes the sonnet's meaning. Instant feedback is a beautiful thing.

Beware, the dreaded *sonnet recitation* elicits more general stress than virtually any other assignment. Generally done early in the year, students universally fear that they will be unable to memorize and recite a sophisticated Shakespearean sonnet. Many believe that they will likely perish in the attempt. When they in fact survive, and often even nail it, their self-esteem rightfully soars. (Shakespeare often brings out the best in students still.) As with the Chapter Master pairs, an assignment such as a sonnet recitation takes a while—and involves little "direct instruction" (that loathsome term). This means that the teacher must surrender control of the process to a great degree. And students must step up and take the stage despite great initial reluctance on the part of many.

Note: most students have substantial fear of public speaking, in part because we do not provide them with opportunities. However, a few kids have genuine phobias. The sensitive teacher must be flexible, strongly encouraging reluctant students, but avoiding situations that could be traumatic. Read their Individualized Educational Programs (IEPs), allow a student to present in private, and make exceptions.

Generally, almost all the kids can and will do it—and oh, the benefits! Kids rise to the challenge, develop quintessential public speaking skills, and assume ownership of their own education as well as that of their peers. This enables the teacher to play a supportive role, rather than the routinely dominant one.

Now we have discussed classroom reading periods, Chapter Masters, and sonnet recitations. It is wise during the 180-day school term to build in blocks of class time in which you are not responsible for creating daily lessons. It varies the pace and the classroom experience, while allowing prep time to be used for grading papers, catching up with bureaucratic #@&*!, preparing for the next unit, or taking a nap by the water somewhere.

Same old same old is a recipe for burnout in any job. So, when students pop into the room with their smiling faces and ask, "What are we doing today?" it's nice to know that they may be excited by the possibilities.

Chapter 2

Why Are We Doing This?

Teachers often assume that students know that the curriculum is inherently valuable. There is an ethic of "Do this, it's good for you." "Eat your vegetables." "Wear a coat outside in winter." "Brush your teeth before you go to bed."

It's a mistake to assume that your students believe that what you are asking, no, *requiring* them to do is valuable to them in the near or far term. The more we sensibly explain the value of what we are doing, the "why," the better. Student buy-in is essential for quality teaching/learning. Motivators are beneficial. Incentives drive human behavior (Levitt and Dubner 2014).

Administrators routinely impose requirements on teachers that are believed to be helpful for promoting more effective learning. These generally last for anywhere from six months to two years, and rarely longer. (Remember Common Core?) They are then replaced by another well-intentioned requirement with the same goal. Teachers are annoyed and frustrated by seemingly endless top-down directives designed to improve us. New things are officially added—and little is ever officially discarded. When the latest initiative is announced, the veteran teachers nod and may even comply to a greater or lesser degree, not getting too worked up, knowing, "This too shall pass."

One thing that our administration directed at one juncture was that we share with students written daily objectives for every lesson. It was likely "New Administrative Requirement of Teachers C-116." Though doing this for every lesson is a bit much, especially if you teach multiple courses and levels, sharing defined objectives and purposes with students is actually a fine concept. It was one that was taken seriously by some of us, and maintained by a few, even as it of course duly fell by the wayside after a relatively brief official existence.

At the beginning of a short story unit (also see Chapter 9), ask the students why reading short stories may have value. They will quickly offer several sound reasons, to which you can add others. That becomes a purpose statement and should be written on the board, or the SMART Board, or poster board, if you don't have any chalkboard space left. Keep it there for the entirety of the unit and refer back to it. It is compelling when students see that we read short stories to

- entertain,
- learn,
- understand other people and places and times and events,
- become more literate,
- increase reading capacity and vocabulary,
- ascertain the differences in writing quality,
- become better able to write stories of our own (as we will do later in the unit), and
- be one with others in the human race.

As for literacy, a slogan utilized for years and mounted prominently in the classroom is "Becoming Highly Literate." Early in the year, students are reminded that they are literate, they can basically read and write. But this year they will attempt to become *highly* literate and will be able to distinguish among various genres and levels of quality. They will hone their research skills. They will become more able to discern the difference between an opinion and an *informed* opinion. They will become far more able to express themselves in speaking and writing. They will become far more adept at reading and listening.

And are these not essential skills? Are these not qualities that often separate successful people from those less successful? (For some of your charges, you may wish to delineate the difference between becoming highly literate and becoming literally high.)

Another effective slogan is "Readers Are Leaders." That too is essential and should be displayed. And a third of this kind is "Writers Are Brighter."

One may be a strong thinker and not a strong writer, but one cannot be a strong writer without being a strong thinker. Teach things of value and offer the attainment of meaningful abilities and virtues. Students will grow to feel more blessed than put upon. (See Zakaria, F., *In Defense of Liberal Education*.)

At the beginning of the year share a document, with your expectations of students clearly delineated. Then offer another document, *What You Can Expect of Your Teacher* (see appendix). Demonstrate that not only do you hold students to high standards of learning, productivity and civility, but you also maintain comparable standards for yourself. We obtain respect as we earn it. And share these documents with parents at open house. (For more on parents, see Chapter 10.)

Then another slogan: "Creating a Community of Scholars." Begin the year with the stated intention that (1) this class will function at a high academic level (scholarship), and (2) we will work collaboratively as a positive powerful group (community). Periodically revisit the expectations and the slogans. Reinforce what you value and honor your own professionalism. Recall for students and yourself the full Henry David Thoreau quote: "In the long run men only hit what they aim at, therefore though they should fail immediately, they ought to aim at something high" (Thoreau 1854).

Have a one- or two-page syllabus that you share with students in the first week and with parents at open house. It describes an emphasis on the four language arts of reading, writing, speaking, and listening (if you teach English and if you don't); major assignments; core objectives; and key readings.

A JOYFUL FIRST DAY

On the first day of school, offer an engaging greeting. Resist the typical listing of rules and distributing a syllabus, seating charts, or anything that is likely to be less interesting. The first day of school is routinely a lost opportunity. Kids come in excited, in new clothes, delighted to see friends, and feeling much older and wiser than the year before. Some are aglow with anticipation, while others are wary, dreading another dull year in school.

There's an alternative to sitting them down, showing them who's boss (as if they don't already know), and handing out material—or worse still, homework on the first day! Instead offer an unexpectedly engaging experience. Welcome them as they arrive and let them sit wherever they wish. (You can always change a seat later if there's an issue.) Say how happy you are to see them and to be with them. Share your own summer experience, let them know they are welcome and special.

Provide colored markers and place cards and have students choose whatever color marker they wish, write their names clearly and place them on their desks or tables facing you. Perhaps highlight a slogan or two that is up on the wall. Ask if anyone else would like to share something special they have done or learned. Then recite a poem or play a wonderful musical work that you love and think they may like—and ask them to free write anything at all in response.

Response journals are of real value. Don't ask them to use their laptops, rather tell the students they can write on paper using pens or pencils, all of which you have in abundance. By their using paper and pen, we avoid unnecessary screen use. Plus, students in many situations still must take major written tests in a paper format, and even penmanship remains important. Never let their not having paper or pencil be an issue. Just let them have as much as they need.

When they ask if you are going to read their responses, the answer should be no. "This is your own journal; you can keep it in a section of a notebook. If you wish me to read it, I am happy to." Expect at least one page of writing single spaced. Write your own response while seated at your desk, again modeling the behavior. Then circulate among them, prompting some to "dig deeper" and produce more words. When most of the kids have approximately one page or more, let them know they should finish up in about a minute.

WRITING FOR THE SAKE OF WRITING

Remember, "writers are brighter," and the more opportunities we provide for free writing the better. There of course should be many graded writing assignments in an English class and several in most other classes as well. At the same time, teachers don't have to grade all student writing. Teachers feeling that they must grade *everything* leads to less student writing and is counterproductive. Writing for its own sake is as meaningful as reading for its own sake, perhaps more so. Sometimes the in-class writing tasks will be more directed than others. Offer students, especially the less capable ones, many options to write freely and uncorrected. This is another potent example of the illusion of choice. Just this simple approach makes writing less onerous for most kids. It also provides a vehicle for those who love to write pages and pages.

Now this is not to say that there isn't value in getting things done, fulfilling requirements, and delaying gratification. A large part of the "why" is that school *is* important. There *is* much to be gained of value by those who commit to the process. The key is to share the current benefits with students and also explain the long-term view, not simply assume they have internalized that. Adolescents are often not particularly good at delaying gratification, but then again neither are a lot of adults. Discipline is a wonderful attribute!

As with other valuable assignments, the Shakespearean sonnet memorization and recitation are rigorous. Advise students upfront that you know a secret method and will tell them. The trick to memorizing the sonnet is . . . memorize it! The trick to reading a classic novel: read it! There is also a secret to saving lots of money: save it! (Of course, you should helpfully share a few other techniques, such as memorizing one quatrain at a time, color-coding or labeling quatrains distinctly, annotating the sonnet for meaning, and so forth.)

Reinforce good habits of mind, good strategies for success. Laud the nerds! Encourage the grinders! And stay on the slackers. Let's face it, 9th grade males are not the most motivated, disciplined, and focused people. Sometime during the 10th grade, and often by 11th, we see a marked change. The light comes on. The looming future is seen as real, rather than a distant mirage. Life after high school is looking more and more likely. What are they going to do?

Now some kids are intrinsically motivated, some are extraordinarily capable, some love school, and some are driven by demanding parents. Upper-middle-class students with successful parents, those in honors and advanced placement classes, student government, varsity captains, and homecoming court members are already on top. Such kids are likely to be fine.

STUDENTS GETTING PAID

Other students may say, "You find this valuable because *you* are getting paid." Respond by saying, "Well, you could be getting paid too—and quite a lot!" The fact is that achieving good grades in high school pays off. And it can pay off handsomely for poorer kids.

Remind your young charges that they too could be getting paid for what they do in high school—in terms of college admission and merit scholarships. Any student with A's in high school can go to a good college. A student with A's and B's can too. When they realize that for each of the forty or so weeks in a school year that they work hard, it can translate into substantial college savings. It's money in the bank. An A student from a middle- or working-class household can receive a "discount" of $40,000 per year, or more, when enrolling in the right private college. Public colleges are less expensive still. That translates to $1,000 per week in savings in high school! Think about it. An A or A-B student can "earn" $200 per day! That's a lot of money. Periodically reminding them of this can be a powerful incentive.

Tell students that in a typical high school course they will garner at least an 85 by (1) simply showing up, (2) doing their homework, and (3) pretending to like the teacher. Participating more fully, doing the homework well, and studying for tests will garner a 90 or better. A functioning student with a decent attitude can "bank" $160K during high school. Again, that's a lot of money. They can all be drawing a handsome salary every day of the school week.

Chapter 3

Teaching to Your Students

Teachers who are admired do not "deliver instruction." Effective teachers engage in teaching/learning with their students. If they are not "learning" it, we are not "teaching" it. And we must be lifelong learners continually modeling that behavior. We may be presenting material, grading quizzes, and assigning homework. We may be working as hard as we can. We should be. At the same time, if half of the kids fail the test it either wasn't a good test or a good time for the test. Toss the results. Admit mistakes every now and then. You'll gain respect, not lose it.

The first thing a teacher forgets is what it is like to be a student. We must continually put ourselves in the student's place. Assume nothing. We usually don't know what happens in that home or on that street, we know little about their diet, sleeping habits, sense of self, family dynamics or history, and even possible patterns of abuse. What we do know is that we must meet them where they are—and take them forward.

Are we the teacher we admired in school? We are unlikely to reach every one of our students—but we are determined to try. And we try not to give up on anyone, ever.

There is ongoing debate as to the merits of various means of grouping students. There is valid concern about access and equity in honors and AP courses, not to mention magnet schools. Affirmative action is a controversial topic. We don't want to simply give students what they haven't earned, what they may not deserve. At the same time, knowing life is developmental and that "you don't want to peak in high school" is equally valid.

Adolescent brains are still developing, in fact, our brains are developing into our twenties (Jensen and Nutt 2015). We must be careful not to create self-fulfilling prophecies when it comes to the young people in our care. Although we can ascertain current levels of ability to some degree, we are less able to factor motivation and background into the equation. Perhaps what we see is more a matter of present performance than innate ability. For we really can't say with any degree of certainty who or what these kids are capable of or may or may not become.

An insightful teacher won't make too many suppositions. We know of many instances where a student who was "never good in English" (or math, or art, or science, or PE) or even hated it, grew to enjoy it, and improve when they had a motivational teacher. The mind and the psyche play huge roles in behavior, expectations, and ultimately performance. Generally speaking, the more we enjoy something, the better we do. Success breeds success. Resist premature judgments—and all judgments are premature with adolescents!

COOPERATIVE LEARNING

Cooperative learning has long been popular, and teachers routinely put kids into groups to work collaboratively. This can have considerable value if done thoughtfully. It can also be pretty much a waste of time if done casually. What do we mean when we say, "cooperative learning"? Surely "learning" must be at the heart of the experience, and that means learning for all.

Early proponents of cooperative learning often recommended a balanced grouping and often of four or even five students. Thus, you might have a strong academic student, a leader, a middling academic student, and a passive kid in the same group (Raebeck 1998).

First let's discuss group size. Appropriate numbers depend upon the assignment. If there are relatively minor tasks of comparable scope and importance, then there can be value in a group of four to five. If there are one or two larger more important tasks and one or two fillers then the group should be smaller. Everyone in the group must have things to do, especially if the group process is going to continue beyond one or two classes. For many activities two–three students per group are fine. Often two is ideal (see next).

In terms of group composition, accept that stronger students are going to have higher expectations and take the task more seriously. Two problems may arise. The first is that the weaker kids may coast and cling to coattails. The second is that the stronger kids grow resentful of this if it happens frequently.

This is also one of the problems with a "group grade" that all members receive. The group grade was a hallmark of original cooperative learning practice. In a large group with task imbalance or vague role descriptors, giving all members the same grade will likely prove unpopular with the kids who are rowing and steering the boat. Determining a fair and unique grade for all group members is also complicated. The recommendation is not to grade any group project. Just eliminate the potential problems. Once students get used to the teacher who doesn't grade everything anyway and the class where lots of ungraded activities are fun and valuable, they won't miss not being graded. They will likely appreciate it (Raebeck 2002). (Note: We will have a wider discussion of assessment in Chapter 8.)

Putting students in pairs is frequently valuable. One of the simplest effective classroom practices is the Pair/Share or "Turn To" (your neighbor). Periodically ask students to discuss with the person next to them and process what they are hearing, reading, writing, or thinking at the moment. This has a genuine immediate impact. You cannot hide in a pair. Within a moment the classroom is buzzing, and most of the pairs stay on task for several minutes. That is all the time needed for this exercise anyway. Other benefits are that students

- take ownership of their learning,
- articulate their views while enhancing their own listening and speaking skills,
- vary the pace of the activity,
- offer a variety of perspectives, and
- provide a break during a teacher-led presentation.

As with larger groups, even with two students in a learning pair it can be tricky. An example of this is with the *Research Project* (which will be discussed in detail in Chapter 9). At one point the thinking was to have two students choose a partner and work together on the lengthy project and resultant paper. They would receive the same grade. This enabled kids to collaborate, and perhaps as importantly, it cut the teacher grading work in half. Reading and grading a lot of five-to-eight-page papers in a decent time frame for providing feedback is challenging. Giving oneself half the load makes wonderful sense.

The problem is that not infrequently, even with either self-selected or teacher-selected pairs, the students will not perform at the same rate or produce the same quality work. Therefore, a single grade is likely to be unfair much of the time. Worse, students may not "rat out" their slacker partners, and the teacher will be guessing as to who did what. So, it may save lots of time, but it is not a good means of assessment. Best to have individual projects and be clear that all students are going through the entire process. You'll just have to grade them all.

EFFECTIVE QUESTIONING

Asking questions of students is central to what we do. The traditional Question and Answer (Q and A) format is ubiquitous in classrooms. Students are generally comfortable with a seminar style and many teachers rely on this approach. Of course, simply doing Q and A does not necessarily enhance teaching/learning. Some strategies are more productive than others.

Open-ended questions are those we do not have a pat answer for. Asking open-ended questions is generally more engaging for students and stimulates higher-level cognition. It is also a way to draw out different types of responses from a wider range of students. Force yourself to ask questions you do not have a definite preconceived answer for.

Asking the date of George Washington crossing the Delaware is a low-level, close-ended question with one answer. Asking, "When Washington led his troops across the Delaware on Christmas Day in 1776, what were some possible outcomes?" is a higher-level, open-ended question with a host of potential responses. And "responses" are often far more interesting than "answers."

When we do this, however, we must wait. Parroting easy answers takes little time. Thinking takes more. Therefore, the deeper the question, the longer we ought to wait for students to formulate thoughtful replies.

You have likely been told before that "wait time" is powerful. Yet there is something about silence in a classroom during Q and A that is unsettling. (All the more so if it is during an administrative observation!) Yet we must wait longer than a second or two if we want our students to intelligently engage with the discussion. And we also must do that in order to facilitate participation from a wider range of students.

Is there an optimal "wait time"? Yes, it should be until some student responds. And that will rarely be longer than a few seconds anyway. Note how long it often takes for an adult to offer the first question at the end of a public lecture or presentation. Yet someone always does, and then the ice is broken.

The low-level question is fodder for the extrovert. Blurting out the "right" answer reinforces that student's sense of stature and dominance while courting teacher approval. Yet the quickest answer is rarely the most thoughtful when dealing with open-ended questions. In fact, it is a sound technique to remind a serial blurter that "I appreciate your participation! Let's hear from someone we haven't heard from yet today." You might even put two to three pencils on a blurter's desk and ask that *he* (likely, though not always) remove one with each of his responses. When the pencils are gone, there can be no more responses from him during that class period.

Socratic seminars offer widespread opportunities for student participation. Crafting eight to ten higher-level guiding questions for the seminar leads to high-level responses. Sharing the questions the day before the seminar provides time for students to digest them. Adequate wait time, especially at the beginning of the activity, promotes thoughtful involvement, as well. Emphasis on broad participation as one of the tenets of an effective seminar will encourage that.

With the teacher acting as facilitator, and not answering any of the questions, every student in the circle potentially may speak. Have two to three of your more extroverted students serve as observers. They can spend their energy charting participation. This alone will provide air time for students less inclined to answer questions in the normal class setting. (During this activity it may also be appropriate at some point to say, "Let's hear from someone we haven't heard from yet.")

Another means of eliciting intelligent responses is to ask students to formulate questions at the beginning of a unit. You may start with having them list what they know about the topic, work, theme, and so on. Then ask them what more they might wish to learn about it. The possibilities are myriad, and students will enjoy the brainstorming experience.

The turn-to exercise, where the teacher stops presenting and asks students to simply speak with a partner seated next to them about what they are learning and thinking, always generates interest. Asking the partner pair to formulate either a statement, a question, or both extends the learning as well.

Finally here, we should note that an element of the Chapter Masters assignment requires that student presenters generate two or three open-ended, higher-level questions of their own. As the conclusion of their presentation, they will ask the class to answer the questions. This is an excellent way to assist students in both understanding and developing higher-level questions—and then offering their peers the opportunity to extend the learning for everyone.

All the while you the teacher may simply encourage and observe. You may also want to pipe up occasionally and demonstrate that you too can answer more sophisticated questions, modeling the desired behavior. Students are happy to hear from a perceptive teacher who doesn't suck all the air out of the room every day.

TEACH TO THE TOP

Effective questioning strategies will offer all manner of students air time. Enabling students to find their voices in a public setting is a gift to them. You are empowering them. And recognizing student differences is as important as treating students fairly and equitably.

When our high school dispensed with the English 10 Honors class there was a widespread concern. The rationale was to broaden access to advanced placement (AP) courses in 11th and 12th grade and so not determine who must be in honors in 10th. Some veteran staff felt that rather than abandon the course, the criteria should be tightened instead, and fewer students admitted, as it had grown to typically include 40 percent or more of the 10th grade population each year. This was in a school of relatively "average" students, most of whom were not going to get a 3 or better on an AP exam later.

Yet the access criteria for honors and APs were lax, and those courses had basically become electives anyway. Students (often pushed by parents) were flocking into the social studies and English 10th grade honors and that weakened the non-honors classes. This created a problem, including a racial one. Our school was quite diverse, with over 50 percent first- and second-generation Latinx, approximately 8 percent Black, and 5 percent native from the local reservation. As APs and honors numbers proliferated, those classes became "whiter," and regular classes became "browner."

When we moved to the new system dispensing with honors English and social studies in 10th grade, the veteran teacher of the 10th grade English honors program decided rather than fight the change, there might be a better way. The plan then became to deliberately "teach up" instead of "teach to the middle." The gamble was to simply use the same curriculum for the mixed group as had been developed for the honors classes. The gamble paid off.

The stronger students, traditionally honors, benefited by being challenged. The middle students generally rose to the challenge. The weaker students struggled to degree but usually made enough effort to progress. As with behavior, having strong and productive kids is a wonderful model for others—as long as they are thriving and not treading water in a less stimulating environment. This notion of "teaching to the top," rather than to the middle, is powerful. Our administration loved the results.

Such a format raises teacher expectations and student productivity. It is ineffective and unfair to lower standards for strong students for the sake of middle and weaker ones. Kids are different. It is essential for public schools to maintain the highest academic standards for all. This is both an educational and political issue. When parents of the more capable students feel that their kids are not being properly challenged or prepared for college they are going to stand up and demand change. We should simply accept that as logical. And the thoughtful open-minded teacher can successfully work with a more diverse group of students.

First, the teacher makes it clear that he or she is fair, wants and expects all students to learn, and cares about each and every student equally. Of course, we subscribe to that theory. But it takes effort to create a classroom that is equitable, supportive, and challenging for virtually all students. Careful selection of materials, methods, responses, and assignments is called for.

The goals are stated in the slogans noted in the last chapter: "Creating a Community of Scholars" while "Becoming Highly Literate." We move toward accomplishing those goals when we individualize teaching/learning through (1) more flexible assessments, (2) varied and engaging experiences, (3) higher-level questioning techniques, (4) extra support for weaker students, (5) a range of creative assignments, and (6) a consistently caring and joyful tone.

Chapter 4

They Will Care for You When You Care for Them

Care is often a marvelous thing, though sometimes a controversial term. While we know intrinsically that we ought to care deeply about our calling and those young people in our charge, there are issues that include rank, age, background, temperament, experience, politics, social mores, roles, gender, institutional protocol, and professional distance.

Let's talk first about "professional distance." As with many other aspects of this notion of being the teacher you admired, balance is key. We cannot be "distant" from our students while expecting them to know we care deeply about them. We must be present. We must be compassionate.

At the same time, we must be perceptive, read cues, and never do anything that makes a student uncomfortable in a personal way. We must probe, but never too deeply. We must challenge, yet recognize individual boundaries and unique personalities. We must be available emotionally while learning the most effective and appropriate ways of doing so. We should try to be a friend, but not a peer. That may need to be stated at times. When a teacher is open to students and treating them well, some students may wish to become too familiar, casual, and even disrespectful. The caring teacher is also careful and sets clear boundaries of language and behavior in the classroom.

One of the unfortunate effects of our ongoing efforts to ensure against sexual harassment is that many teachers are now afraid to even touch students with a tap on the shoulder or the head or the hand. Humans need human touch—of the right kind. A student in stress may be crying out for kindness, for reassurance, and for comfort. Trauma is all around us. Students lose parents and grandparents, see pets die, suffer parental divorce, have their hearts broken, get sick, have debilitating injuries, and endure devastating losses and tragedies. Some become suicidal. It happens all the time when we are dealing with large numbers of kids.

The loving teacher knows powerful and fully appropriate ways to support kids in stress. Over time, one's reputation will be accurate. If you are a caring, open, and ethical teacher who sincerely loves your work and your students, others will come to know and value that, including peers, counselors, parents, and administrators. At the same time, it is incumbent on the responsible adult to create safe classroom spaces and foster in your students the awareness that you can be trusted.

TEACHER AS COUNSELOR

When you are open to your students, they will come to you with all manner of issues. The caring teacher is aware that when a student is struggling academically or behaving inappropriately there is likely a problem lurking. When we maintain "professional distance," however, students are unlikely to come to us for help, and they are not going to reveal circumstances that are painful, embarrassing, or debilitating. Some teachers understandably prefer it that way. The teacher who is unwilling to notice that students are in need or at-risk misses opportunities to serve those kids in a meaningful way. Yes, we may leave that to counselors, administrators, and support staff. The problem is that kids may feel equally reluctant to confide in those people too. When they learn that you are an adult who cares and maybe even can help, you are in a position to fulfill a vital role in your school community.

Once students begin to realize that you are there for them, that you care at least as much for them as people than as students, they will be open to an inquiry as to their emotional state. "How are you?" actually means "*How* are you?" They may even seek you out. Simply finding time for a one-on-one meeting with a troubled student is the first step. In that meeting in a classroom or office, the first step is to gently listen. Refrain from judgment, condescension, scolding, or even giving advice. Just listen, asking encouraging questions. Young people are quite good at getting to the point—especially when they know you care.

A trusted adult is a tremendous resource for a struggling young person trying to find their way. The educator and psychologist William Glasser developed *Choice Theory* (Glasser 1985). From that came *Reality Therapy*, which is remarkably cogent and effective. The gist of this approach is that intrinsic motivation is far more powerful psychologically than extrinsic. The most important human needs are love and belonging, as closeness and connectedness with the people we care about provide ultimate satisfaction.

Therefore, we must practice caring habits of support, encouragement, acceptance, trust, respect, listening, and negotiating differences. We must avoid criticizing, blaming, complaining, nagging, threatening, punishing, and bribing or rewarding to control another.

The emphasis is on the three Rs of Reality, Responsibility, and Right and wrong. We must learn to determine that what is real is our willingness to accept the consequences of our actions. Responsibility is meeting one's own needs without infringing on the rights of others. And right and wrong is something you typically know by how you feel. Understanding and applying the basis of *Reality Therapy* with students will make you far more effective both in teaching and counseling.

Of course, you are not going to solve large problems in fifteen or thirty minutes—though you may solve lesser problems looming in the mind of an anxious teen. Be flexible and willing to consider individual situations. Allow for extra time to hand in an assignment. Modify an assignment for a student who is overwhelmed by work that is due in other classes. Cut deals. You will gain respect, not lose it when kids see that you listen, are kind, and considerate.

When the problem is greater, additional steps are required. You will hear about heartbreak, stress at home, poverty, alcoholic parents, abusive relationships, self-harm, eating disorders, exhaustion from working after school and on weekends because the family needs money, or that the family must move because the rent is unpaid. This is when your student needs still more help. Will you offer it? Will you follow up with guidance and administration, speak with the school psychologist or social worker? Call a parent when that is necessary?

The teacher who is available on a deeper level may sense, or be told, that this kid is in danger of self-harm of the dreaded "s" word, suicide. Suicide in general and teenage suicide in particular is a growing problem in our country.

According to the National Institute of Mental Health, teen suicide increased 32.4 percent between 1999 and 2019 (NIMH 2020). The perceptive teacher must ask a student in stress if that tragic act is possible, if it has been considered or even attempted. You may find that the answer is "yes"—and no one else, *no one else*, knows of this. That is when you offer your cell phone number and say, "You *must* call me if you are thinking dark thoughts. Any time, day or night, weekend, whatever. I am here for you." And tell them you are bound to report this to the administration and do so at once. You may be saving a life.

An effective conversation may include a pep talk. After you have provided ample time for the students to share everything and anything on their minds, draw from your own well. Encourage them that they can get through this. Share difficulties of your own in high school. Pay them a genuine compliment or two, whether it is their sense of humor, popularity with peers, writing ability, or hairstyle. Note their strengths and positive circumstances, a "glass is half full" approach. Often when we are in despair we focus exclusively on our deficits, forgetting our assets.

We also may feel that we are "looking up a mountain" impossibly steep. Break their problem into manageable parts, a "journey of a thousand miles begins with a single step." Ask them what they can do right now, today, to assume responsibility and regain some sense of control of their own well-being. Plan for a follow-up meeting within a day or a week, depending on the issue. Tell them that you believe in them. Tell them that you have worked with countless other suffering teens who ultimately made it. Say that you were one of those teens. End on a positive note of promise and renewal. It will likely take more than this, but a sincere pep talk from a caring teacher *can* transform a life.

To summarize the pep talk:

- Listen
- Encourage
- Share a difficulty from your own adolescence
- Pay a compliment or two
- Remind the student of their assets
- Offer a first simple step forward
- Schedule a follow-up meeting within the next few days

- State/restate your faith in them
- Note that you know many other kids who struggled yet prevailed
- Volunteer that you are one of those kids

Having such an impact on your students is not entirely selfless, by the way. We gain tremendously when we see that we are helping others. Knowing that you are a valuable person in your school is gratifying. It can add years of meaning to a professional career that is often difficult, tedious, and undervalued. Better to come home at the end of the day with the satisfaction that not only have you helped kids learn important things, you have provided hope and love.

VARY YOUR ROLES

Teachers often take on additional duties as coach, club advisor, play director, after-school support, and so on. Yes, the extra money is welcome, though it generally isn't much. As important is the opportunity to share other facets of yourself outside of the classroom—and see your students in different ways as well. Those roles are generally less formal and provide chances to be fun and collaborative with kids. It also expands access, as students not necessarily in your classes may join an activity you are leading.

Often young teachers without children of their own engage more in extracurriculars and then less so as they grow older. Yet continuing to participate in the life of the school community beyond the classroom has value. Building a new program in an area your school lacks can also be wonderful for certain students with interest and talent there. Start a chess club, a literary and arts magazine, a school newspaper, a videography program, a new sport, or a yoga club; direct a play; plant a garden; and create an art group. Do something special for the school and expand your own capabilities and interests in the process.

RECOMMENDATIONS

When you are an effective teacher, high school students will ask you for recommendations. This is yet another extra role to assume, and it is not easy.

The more successful your students are, and the more accessible you are, the more that kids will ask you to provide written support in the college or job application process. Writing a strong recommendation requires knowledge of the student, proficient writing skills, compassion, and understanding of what colleges and employers wish to know. The key is a balance of what the student has accomplished academically in your class, something he or she has done of value outside the classroom, and who the student is in terms of ethics and relationships. This may not be so difficult for one or two seniors a year. If dozens of kids are asking, including underclassmen wishing for a special recognition or opportunity, then it can become daunting and tedious.

One technique that will greatly simplify this for you is to establish a template for male and female students in each of your classes. Within that you define the major curricular tasks and learnings, as well as a paragraph for the student's extracurricular experience and leadership, and then one for the student's moral compass, peer relationships, community service, and so on. Once those are established, it is not time consuming to ask for a resume or activities sheet and customize the text for an individual. This technique will enable you to write effective recommendations in a matter of fifteen-thirty minutes.

An admirable teacher plays a vital role in the lives of students. We are all seeking connection and purpose. We are all seeking respect and support, challenge and fulfillment. Relationships are central to human experience. The effective teacher is willing and able to offer students mentoring, kindness, strength, and joyfulness. What's more, fostering such friendships offers gratification unknown in many professions. Embrace it. Caring for our students is the heart of our responsibility. And how they do appreciate it and care for us in return!

Chapter 5

Sit Down and Shut Up
Secrets of Classroom Management

Ah, classroom management—another key ingredient to the sauce of joyful teaching. No matter how caring, committed, knowledgeable, and organized you may be, you must be in command.

There was once a worthy educator whose first observation, that by his matronly and solemn department head, was horrific. It was early in the term, in an "average" class of rambunctious 10th graders, led by a nasty oversized and overaged ringleader. The youthful teacher would surely have preferred his sweet little sophomore honors class for the initial observation, but that was not to be.

Many rookie mistakes were made. He thought that if he told the kids about the observation and asked for their support it would be cheating. He had several activities planned but was less certain of how long they might last. As the observation came on the heels of the prior class, he had yet to write the requisite instructions on the board (not even thinking of printing them up beforehand and distributing them instead). Finally, he failed to introduce the guest, sitting silently in a rear corner of the room. The students were unaware of her stolid presence.

Things did not get off to a propitious start. Trying desperately not to sweat so profusely that puddles might pool below him, he had nearly finished writing the task on the board when an awful sound was heard behind him. It was akin to that made by a smaller mammal being bitten by a larger one.

Turning abruptly, he saw an astonishing sight. His best, most conscientious and capable student had nearly lost his head—or so it appeared. Four brigands each held a leg of the diminutive Andrew's desk, and they had rather easily hoisted it aloft. His head had hit the fragile ceiling tile suspended on the metal frame above and pushed the tile upward to allow entry. Andrew's head was disappearing.

Again, doing everything humanly possible to appear in control, our erstwhile rookie managed to hiss a harsh command: "Put him down!" For some still unknown reason, the villains stopped their deviltry, snickered, and began lowering Andrew back to earth. As the stunned adolescent resumed a stationary position, the teacher motioned with scrunched up eyebrows toward the back of the classroom. Silently he implored the group to recognize that there was a visitor among them. Within a few moments most of them had done so. And for some blessed reason they were far better behaved during the remainder of the lesson.

Our young pedagogue lost sleep prior to his post-observation meeting the next day. He was certain that it would be the beginning of a series of negative reviews, likely culminating in criminal charges and ignominious dismissal before the December holiday break. But that also was not to be. For whatever reason, perhaps experience, patience, or even sympathy, his department chair produced a generally favorable report. Within it she did note, however, that his classroom management might be somewhat more effective with time and effort.

STUDENT MORALE

Ahh, classroom management. It's not as simple as posting a sign saying, "The beatings will continue until morale improves." It does come back to the notion of creating a community of scholars. One central aspect of a functional and respectful classroom is offering a variety of engaging experiences. We're more likely to get and hold attention when the process is enjoyable and meaningful. Emphasizing the *why* along with the *what* and *how* is key.

Thinking in terms of "student morale" in your classroom and in the school overall is more productive than thinking in terms of "discipline" or "control." Is your classroom a haven, a safe space, a respite from a larger, haphazard, and even frightening world for many of your students? Is your classroom a mecca? Or is it simply a place to kill time, a place to play school? Or far worse, is it just one more brick in the wall?

The joyful teacher sees the classroom as an oasis of purposeful teaching/learning, good vibes, support, and cooperation. Going there every workday should feel more like a pleasure than a burden.

Another basic in such artfulness is balance. Artful teachers

- know what is going on in the classroom,
- move around in that space regularly and comfortably,
- are friendly and helpful,
- interact with as many students as possible during each class, and
- continually say hello to students in the hallway and cafeteria.

The effective teacher also conveys what is acceptable and what is not—on a regular basis. This involves consequences rather than punishments and responses rather than reactions. It's helpful to remind yourself that you are living and working with adolescents, and thus you will see adolescent behavior. Say, "You know, you are acting like sophomores in high school!" They will reply earnestly, "We *are* sophomores in high school." Being playful and understanding goes a long way.

"Selective hearing" is valuable. There is a difference between (1) some beleaguered kid already having a bad day muttering an expletive just loud enough to be heard and (2) some belligerent kid cursing to challenge the teacher and get attention. In the first case, ignoring it is best. In the second, it may only require, "Please don't use that language in this class." To assign detention or write up a high school student for cursing once in a class is an overreaction. People curse quite regularly, and it begins in elementary and middle school. Although it can be excessive, obnoxious, and profoundly unnecessary, there are greater threats to civilization.

A wonderful ancient Chinese proverb of Chuang Tzu's is called "The Empty Boat."

> If a man is crossing a river
> And an empty boat collides with his own skiff,
> Even though he be a bad-tempered man
> He will not become very angry.
> But if he sees a man in the boat,
> He will shout at him to steer clear.
> If the shout is not heard, he will shout again.

And yet again, and begin cursing.
And all because there is somebody in the boat.
Yet if the boat were empty,
He would not be shouting, and not angry.

If you can empty your own boat
Crossing the river of the world,
No one will oppose you,
No one will seek to harm you. (Merton 2004)

Deal with problems before they escalate. Much of this is subjective and intuitive. Your classroom management will be more effective when there is a clear philosophy motivating it. Offer respect before expecting or demanding it. Be willing to laugh at yourself. Surrender the need to be fully in control and gradually you may have more of it. Lead by example. Be an effective listener. Constantly remind yourself why you are a teacher—and how wonderful it can be.

STARTING CLASS CALMLY

It is common school pedagogy to start class promptly and productively. Off and running at the bell! But secondary school students are not thoroughbreds. Even if they were, they likely wouldn't prosper by running eight to ten races each day.

As we know, the school day is exhausting and relentless. Offering kids a break at the beginning of class pays dividends, despite the conventional wisdom about the quick engaging start of "the lesson." We know that kids (especially girls) barely, or don't, have enough time to go to the bathroom between classes. They race to class to be on time, then ask to go to the restroom. That is woefully inefficient for the class, as well as needlessly embarrassing for the student.

Instead, let it be known informally that they can arrive a minute or so after the bell without penalty. And let those already there just chill. Chat with their friends, ask you a question, hand in an assignment, get a drink of water, put their phones away. And you can take partial attendance, hand back papers, check your email, catch up with a student, make a cup of coffee, speak to a passing colleague, and share a moment.

Four or five minutes is not enough time to reset between classes—for the students or the teacher. Six or seven works better. And when it is time to begin, everyone will be more ready.

DOMINANT POSITIVES AND DOMINANT NEGATIVES

In groups there often is a dominant personality. And groups often take on the personality of the dominant person. If the dominant kid in a class is a DP, Dominant Positive, that's good. That alone will lead to far fewer behavior issues and higher morale. If the dominant person is a DN, Dominant Negative, things will be more difficult initially.

Early in the year you will know who the DP or DN is. Cultivating a relationship with that student is imperative. Of course, it is likely to be harder to cultivate a positive relationship with a DN. Moving forward with the assumption that everyone needs to be loved, especially a miserable bully, start working right away on changing the student–teacher dynamic that kid has come to expect. Remember, no student *wants* to be in trouble. No one wants to fail, though some students may appear to not care at all about success when success has long proven elusive.

Don't overreact when he or she pushes your buttons. Assume selective hearing when it makes sense. Ask the DN academic questions or to read one of the class slogans, in an attempt to engage in intellectual discourse, offering a positive way of getting teacher and peer attention. Avoid any sarcasm or hostility, even if provoked.

Find a time in the first week, if possible, to chat outside of class time—before there is a problem or needs to be a consequence for unacceptable behavior. In that five-minute chat at your desk or in some suitable spot, share something positive about the student and emphasize that you are excited about the year and happy to be the teacher. Then ask if there is anything you can do to help that kid be successful.

That may be enough to get things moving in the right direction. It is also quite possible that you can't win the DN over so easily. When the conflict comes and the confrontation looms, do not get upset or angry in front of the class. Quietly ask the student to step outside into the hallway with you and then move away from the door. Take a deep breath. Say in a calm voice, "Are you okay? Is there something going on that has you upset? Can I help?

Would you like to take a few moments out here to calm down? Go get a drink of water? What can we do to have a better experience in our class today? I really want this to work."

Notice: no threats, no punishments, no use of the ineffectual, "Why are *you* behaving like this?" Use Haim Ginnot's "I messages," saying "I" more and "you" less (Study.com 2022). No public putdown or confrontation. Use time and space as allies. Remind yourself that you are the adult and have tools forged over many years.

Another plus in this simple action of "stepping outside" is that the other students see you taking charge of the situation—but they have no idea what you and the DN did or didn't say in the hall. If it works, you will come back in the class about as together as when you stepped out, and either then or a little bit later the difficult student will also return and go to his or her seat.

Many teachers rarely write up students to refer them to administration for discipline. Some never do. Others do it constantly. Usually, a handful of teachers make the majority of referrals to the assistant principal. They are dealing with pretty much the same student population yet having entirely different results. It's usually not the kids.

A disciplinary referral should be a teacher's last resort, not the first one. Is it smart to fire a worker at the first mess-up? Isn't that a last resort? When you write up a student, you are ostensibly saying to the administrator, "I can't or won't deal with this kid." And then the same teacher who does that routinely second guesses the administrative action, often feeling it is too lenient. Many secondary schools have a cadre of teachers complaining that the administration is not "hammering the kids." Is school meant to be more punitive or educational?

There are so many methods we can employ prior to the disciplinary referral. We have noted several earlier. In addition, provide clear directions, engaging activities, variety, humor, care, paper and pencils, and additional copies of the novel, text, or essay being studied. It's unrealistic to expect twenty-five or thirty kids to *all* have *all* their stuff every day.

When trouble emerges anyway, as it surely will at times, we also need interventions. Use positive reinforcement, note a student or students who are in learning mode and ready, move close to the student's seat, lightly touch a forearm, restate a class slogan, goal, or expectation, and offer an invitation to "see me after class" (SMAC) without saying precisely what it may entail. In a hotter spot do the hallway visit.

Sometimes simply changing the student's seat can alter the classroom dynamic. That is best done at the beginning of a class period, not right after "a situation" during class. Changing seats demonstrates you are in control, especially if you initially allow kids to sit wherever they wish, which is fine.

It's also important to remember that the struggling students generally seek the rear of the class and the corners in the traditionally configured classroom. They avoid the Power T, the central seats in the front rows, knowing that teachers pay far more attention to students in those most visible spots. Put the little darlin' front and center, right under your nose. You may not like it, but you'll like it more than a constant distraction in the far corner. And it is quite possible that in time the miscreant will like having your attention without doing something wrong. It is quite possible that you will transform an enemy into an ally.

Outside of class there are other things to do, of course. Become familiar with the student's file and IEP if applicable. Talk to other teachers, guidance counselors, support staff, and administrators. Call home to make the parental connection—and best to do so without having or mentioning a particular problem. Frame the call as one of care and assistance. Parents of DNs are fully aware their cherub is no prize in school. They often will welcome your sincere help. They are no happier about school problems than their child is. Be part of the solution.

It's important to be idealistic *and* realistic, practicing "pragmatic idealism." There will likely be students who are incorrigible, disturbed, and even dangerous. Developing a reputation for being kind, fair, and effective with your students happens over time if you are such a teacher. Then, when confronted with a student problem that appears insoluble after your best efforts, taking it to administration and guidance is fine.

Over years, even the strongest teachers may have a few kids they cannot reach. There is a tipping point where the teacher must opt for the greater good. The deeply troubled student should not be permitted to keep other students from learning or the teacher from teaching. We are not giving up on the problematic individual, but we are saying that this particular setting may not be appropriate. It is no longer fair to all the others impacted so negatively.

Perhaps simply switching the student to another teacher or different set of peers will help.

That point of serious intervention should not be reached quickly or casually. It may come, however, and a conscientious administrator will support a caring teacher.

This is a lengthy list of strategies for successful classroom management, for creating a community of scholars. Incorporating these into your modus operandi will pay dividends. The successful joyful teacher is reflective. Maintain ongoing reflections, such as "Is this working?" and "What can I do to make things better?"

Yes, this takes time—and loads of energy. There are few professions that require as much human energy as teaching does when done well. Enhancing student morale while dealing with all your kids fairly and joyously is as important an effort as a teacher can make. The satisfaction that comes as a result will help to refill your bucket. We never lose by giving.

Chapter 6

The Classroom as a Home

Just as an organization over time reflects the personality of the leader, so does a classroom reflect the attitude and approach of the teacher. Think about the kind of classroom you enjoyed being part of when you were in school. Most public school classrooms are approximately the same shape and size, most have one door to a hallway, windows to the outside world (or at least the parking lot), a clock on the probably cinder block wall, chalkboards/ smartboards, a teacher desk, and desks for the kids lined up in five or six rows of five or six desks each. Beyond that there may or may not be a great deal of variety.

Of course, not all teachers have their own classrooms and many must share. However, many veteran teachers can basically call one classroom space their own and most have some flexibility in how it is arrayed and equipped. As a teacher grows more comfortable and capable in the profession and more attuned to the needs of students, the classroom should reflect that.

When one thinks of the classroom as a *home* (for the teacher, and at least as importantly, for the students who spend time there) that space cannot simply be left in a stark, uninviting, and nearly identical mode to other classrooms. Just as a school ought to in theory be a place that students would actually come to if they weren't required, so a classroom should be a haven and a comfort so that kids will enjoy being there when they have an assigned class and may even hang out there when they don't. Much of this will be due to the personality and attitude of the teacher, yet that attraction can be enhanced with furniture, equipment, and decorations.

COMFORTABLE FURNITURE

The first thing is to move away from the rows and desks as much as possible and bring in furniture that is comfortable and accommodating. Tables and chairs, in some varied shapes and types, allow students choice and a measure of independence. This will prove far more inviting than the hard, inflexible, relatively small desks that all size and shape of students are forced into all day every day. Then add a couch or two, if you dare.

Some less flexible folks, including some typical administrators, will feel terribly threatened by a change in the layout and even the *thought* of couches. Kids asleep! Kids making out! Instruction suffering. Discipline dying. Please, it's a couch, not a waterbed! Students will get to class early to claim a spot on it. You can put it front and center, instantly changing the seating dynamic and getting some of your most mischievous students to class on time and sitting right under your nose voluntarily. Two couches simply double the effect.

Then the lighting: get lamps and use them and the natural light from the windows and leave the overhead fluorescent lights turned off—we are not growing basil in a hydroponic greenhouse. The result will be relaxing, even calming, and students will enjoy the difference, often without realizing it. But do get lamps. A teacher who doesn't use the overhead lights, but has a dark classroom is trading one problem for another. Don't ask the administration for standing floor lamps, just go out and buy them yourself for $20–30.

The issue of physical comfort cannot be overstated. We take care of some of that with flexible and pleasing seating, as well as soothing and appropriate lighting. What about temperature and airflow? Most school systems believe that allowing individual teachers to control their classroom HVAC will lead to socialism and then anarchy. That's nonsense of course. However, with the use of windows, doors, shades, fans, and even portable AC units, classrooms can be made far more comfortable.

Okay, so while you're at Walmart, get a microwave, a coffee maker, and a small fridge. Great investments! Then buy a few cleaning supplies. Stop at the market for some coffee and sugar and cream, maybe fruit juice or cereal and milk. You'll have snacks and coffee when you need it, hot food when you want it—and you won't have to waste time going elsewhere.

Then you'll need music for yourself and for your students. With a SMART Board and YouTube that's easy enough these days. Playing music that the kids like is a wonderful way to deepen your connection with them and also make your classroom more inviting. One nice thing these days is that adolescents generally enjoy all kinds of music that's good, not simply the most recent. However, the cool teacher knows that good music did not stop with Chuck Berry, R.E.M., Sinead O'Connor, or anyone else. An occasional film that is excellent is also a perfectly fine use of time, as long as it is occasional. Kids see a lot of videos these days, as previously noted.

But don't stop yet in making your classroom a home. What else do kids need on a regular basis? Outlets to charge their devices, pens and pencils, paper, extra copies of texts, stories, essays, whatever you are using.

Oh, and books, lots of books. Of course, there are always classroom sets of texts or novels. Maintaining a lending library facilitates student reading. Obtaining worthy books of many types and applicable reading levels is not difficult. Having a wide range of excellent books is helpful when a student is looking for a book for the *Book Non-Report* or just a free read. (See chapters 1 and 9 for information on the *BNR*.) A student will show up and say that a friend is happily reading *Pride and Prejudice*. How nice to be able to simply hand out another copy.

Book fairs, supply closets, used book stores, and your own living room are all places to obtain books for your classroom. Having an in-class library models reading behavior while adding to the homey feel of your classroom. Just don't expect all the books to come back!

Then there is the wide expanse of wall space, generally blandly painted cinder block. It can serve as a major exhibit space, and there is no shortage of fun, inspiring, artistic, cool, intriguing posters and placards, signs and slogans, and other things to put up, including student projects and their works of art. Whenever you travel bring back souvenirs and mementos and pictures for the room, your Museum of International Culture. And every time you add something new, ask the kids to spot it. Let them learn by looking.

Then we can add plants and a watering can, bringing another form of organic life into the space. And let's not forget photographs. First, yours—friends, children, spouse, and parents. What a generous means of sharing your world. Then you can also have students periodically take photos of the kids in the class doing all manner of things, or nothing special, just being there. Get them printed on Snapfish or whatever. Set up a cork board and display as many such photos as you can—and the kids will love it. They will implore you to get photos of them, if they aren't already there, or their class isn't, if only prior years are on the cork boards. Those photo displays of current and former students will prove as appealing to kids as anything in your room.

Thinking in terms of a physically and emotionally healthy environment, we want to minimize distractions and maximize focus and care for what we are doing at the moment. Fighting for focus in a public secondary school is a constant battle (as noted previously with Ms. Martinet). Creating relative quiet in the classroom, whether for silent independent reading, essay writing, or listening to a poetry recitation by the teacher or a student is an ongoing struggle. There are many times in such a setting where a dedicated teacher comes to believe that the entire system is conspiring against quiet, focus, genuine learning, and meaningful human interaction.

This means that an admirable teacher does not give in to the madness. A professional educator continually defines his or her teaching/learning time and space. That may require closing the door, drawing the shades, silencing the PA system, disconnecting the school phone (as well as shutting off everyone else's), shushing noisy people in the halls or next door, insisting on not being interrupted unnecessarily by kids, other teachers, clerical and custodial staff, and administrators. Often it only takes a stern glance. (Though brandishing a stout object can also prove effective.) Being known as a curmudgeon may be a small price to pay for having an uninterrupted and focused teaching/learning space at least some of the time.

Not only are classroom walls stark and hard, so are floors, generally of polished tile. They are loud, echoing, and unpleasant to sit on. Utility trumps comfort once again. So, get some carpet, some remnants, some underlayment, and place that in the classroom. Carpet absorbs sound and every now and again people may actually sit on it. Teenagers are not that far removed from childhood and welcome returning to a childlike state free of the anxieties of their current one.

Each year before the December holiday have kids bring in picture books they loved when little and you can bring in your favorites too. Sitting on the carpet in a circle and taking turns reading those stories aloud while sharing the illustrations, as though you were all back in kindergarten, is a blessed activity. It may even feel like home.

Chapter 7

The Classroom as a Theater

Speaking of blessed activities, the engaging teacher is an accomplished actor. And not everything has to be serious and purposeful, even if the overall intention is for genuine lasting learning. Enlivening the day-to-day with unexpected, delightful, preposterous, hilarious, and extraordinary experiences is valuable in its own right. A student in an anticipatory state is one with an open mind and a vital brain. Offering novelties, pranks, high jinks, and playfulness will be endlessly welcome. Fun is a great ally of learning (Levitt and Dubner 2014).

Offering extraordinary experiences comes with risk. This is a logical reason that some teachers are overly conventional, not to say boring. It is easier and safer to stay inside the box. This is true in many professions, and education is one of the more conservative ones. But no adult sings the praises of their most conventional and boring secondary school teachers, do they?

There are two things to bear in mind when attempting to become a good teacher and even a great one. There has to be equilibrium in your classroom. If you are exciting and spontaneous and compelling and wonderfully eccentric you still have to be focused, rigorous, and purposeful. Effective administrators welcome effective teaching, over time. They will be supportive of your unconventionality, or at least tolerant, so long as they see solid and consistent teaching/learning in your program. Parents will respond comparably, over time.

The second key is that you must be continually monitoring your impact on your students. Some pranks are better than others, as are quips, comments, mannerisms, and attitudes. Nothing you do should ever hurt a student. And in the current political landscape, that can be tricky.

Teasing has gotten a bad rap lately. Some adults believe that basically all kids, even at fifteen or sixteen or seventeen, are incredibly fragile. But playful teasing can also be a way of connecting with someone and even solidifying their place in the group. There is a big difference between playful teasing and sadistic bullying on the spectrum of human interaction (PREVNet 2022). Effective teachers are not afraid of playful teasing and are also willing to absorb their share. At the same time, effective teachers ensure that in their classrooms kids are respected and protected. Once that is established, there is room for theatrics. Let the show begin!

PROPS: THE GOLDEN GOLF CLUB AND THE STEEL ROD

In the preface we referred to the Golden Golf Club and its usefulness in hitting clementines out the window. All that is required is a seven iron or some such lofted club and a can of gold spray paint. Once the club is gilded, bring it into the class. It is essential to tell students just how expensive a solid gold golf club is (approximately $50,000 at today's prices). It's also essential to obtain their agreement not to divulge to *anyone* that there is such an expensive item sitting in a corner or unlocked closet in a classroom in the school.

Assuming you have even modest golfing ability, you need not be limited to clementines—though they are a perfect substitute for a golf ball. Striking many an organic object with a golf club offers spectacular results. Though careful aim should lead to at least some of the fruit, such as the core or pit, going toward the target (ideally a large sliding window), fragments of the body will go in all other directions. Vegetable matter could plant itself on furniture, shelving, desks, windows, books, backpacks, ceiling tiles, floor, clothing, and humans, including the golfer. Over time one learns to cover things with plastic, drop covers or steel-plated tank armor, and clear aside potential collateral damage (students) prior to the decisive blow.

Among items to consider as projectiles are oranges, grapefruits, bell peppers, bananas, apples, tomatoes (no, *not* tomatoes), and large mushrooms preferably picked from the school lawn. (Yes, that has happened. The result: a miniature mushroom cloud.)

Although it is a wise policy not to permit the use of cell phones (previously discussed), an exception can be made for the filming of this display. Hitting a cell phone out the window would be super cool too. Uh, no. (See "some pranks are better than others" above.)

Another prop that may be utilized to great effect is the Steel Rod. This can be easily obtained in a standard file cabinet. The rods used in drawers to hang file folders are perfect. The Steel Rod is a wonderful AGD (Attention Getting Device).

We live in an era of endless student rights and protections, with corporal punishment in schools a distant memory to geriatrics. The effective educator still requires a tool or two to pretend to maintain control. A Steel Rod is just such a tool. Brandishing the rod every now and again, or slapping it on a desk, will produce undivided attention. Merely striding back and forth in front of the class while pounding the Rod into one's palm will produce unwarranted respect. To increase your impact, add strong language in a disciplinary tone with a foreign accent.

There was once a teacher who became envious of certain male students' skill at impaling pencils in the ceiling tiles when he wasn't watching or wasn't present between periods. He would enter the classroom to find more than a few stuck in the ceiling, rather than placed in the pencil box. He implored the miscreants to show him how to do this fancy trick. But try as he might, he was unable to get even one to stick there. Voila, the Steel Rod.

"I'll show you!" he thought to himself. Balancing his body like a cat on a tree limb, he gripped the Rod deftly in his right hand. Then, whoosh! Into the ceiling it went—and so remained. The students knew that they had been bested once again.

CAUTIONARY NOTE

One ought to know what to say, and not say, to parents at open house. That is not always clear to theatrical types.

At an open house an eccentric teacher revealed that one of his props was an actual dunce cap. A large piece of white drawing paper had been furled into a cone shape and on it in French was written "Le Chapeau de Le Dunce." It sat proudly on a file cabinet likely bereft of at least one steel rod. The foolish teacher lightheartedly told the parental audience that he wore the cap sometimes for the students' amusement. And he said he periodically placed the dunce cap on the heads of various students. He also noted that students clamored to be the one so designated. There were even photos of a few particularly photogenic dunces on the student pictures cork boards.

The next day the assistant principal solemnly warned our thespian that a parent had complained. Best to discard Le Chapeau de Le Dunce, he was told. And so he did—for the remainder of that term or the tenure of the assistant principal, whichever was the shortest.

URNS, ASHES, INTERNAL FIELD TRIPS, GUMBY, AND MOTHER SUPERIOR

Should one be an English teacher one may wish to share the marvelous odes of John Keats. Should one choose "Ode on a Grecian Urn," one might wish to have a ceramic vessel of some kind as an example. A large flowerpot may serve, and perhaps there may still be some potting soil within it.

Once upon a time, a theatrical sort was expounding on the properties of an urn and brought just such a large flowerpot off an upper shelf. There was indeed old dried potting soil in the now flowerless pot. Without thinking more, the teacher held up a handful of the dry stuff and claimed that it was the ashes of his dear departed grandfather. The students naturally decried this as impossible, especially due to the excessive amount of "ashes" in the large size pot. "He was a big man at the end" was the answer to their doubting.

Students love field trips if for no other reason than they get to leave school during school time. Yet lots of teachers resist field experiences in part because they use precious class time—their own and that of their peers.

The *Internal Field Trip* can be a remedy for the student-teacher conflict. First, it is done during one class period, so that it doesn't interfere with anyone else's program. Second, it is unexpected and extraordinary. Third, it need not involve any planning, money, or larger purpose. Often a simple trip to the cafeteria suffices, for at almost any time many kids are going to be hungry, if not voraciously so.

Remind the students that they can demonstrate one of the primary takeaways from elementary school—the class walking in an orderly and relatively silent line through the halls. Ask for a line leader and have everyone else buddy up, even holding hands if they wish. Of course, the girls will be much more likely to hold hands.

The copy room is another legitimate destination. The principal's office probably not.

It is supremely worthwhile just to see the expressions on the faces of people in the corridors or cafeteria as the teacher-led troupe marches proudly past. "*We* are taking an internal field trip."

Although the possibilities for mischief are endless, Gumby is a marvelous partner-in-crime (PIC). For those who may not know of him, Gumby is a six-inch, green, rubber, toy man based on a cartoon character. Pokey is his red horse, comparably sized so that Gumby may ride him if he so chooses. Gumby has a perpetual smile, and nothing can change that beatific expression. Although he is rubber and his mouth is only painted on, sometimes he will speak in his high-pitched lilting voice. Yet it is not possible to determine in advance what he will say—nor to stop him from doing so, even at inopportune moments. Plus, Gumby is known to be quite the wise guy and routinely insults teachers and students. He is incorrigible.

The best way to keep him somewhat in line is to threaten to hit him out the window with the Golden Golf Club. This will elicit from him first groans—and then even shouts, threats, and imprecations. However, once he is teed up, he finally shuts up, and out he goes! Beyond the beauty of finally silencing his obnoxious voice is that no matter where he winds up—on the floor, smashed against the window, sitting in the grass outside, or even on the pavement in the front drive after being run over by a student driver—he will be smiling. His unmoved demeanor is a testament to the positive attitude required for such resilience. We can all learn a great deal from Gumby.

Finally, we can also learn a great deal from the world's most beloved musical, *The Sound of Music*. The show is full of life lessons delivered in a delightful, yet powerful, way. Film versions of great musical comedies, such as this one and *My Fair Lady*, for example, will prove a wonderful cultural experience for students, and many have not ever seen them.

To enhance the value, the effective teacher can become an accomplished vocalist mastering multiple roles. An especially memorable impact comes from singing "Climb Evr'y Mountain." That song is forcefully sung early on and then as a refrain in *The Sound of Music* by the mother superior character. Few lessons will prove more compelling to your students than offering your version of "Climb Evr'y Mountain," perhaps right before a mid-term or final exam.

Chapter 8

Highly Effective Assessment

A book about joyful teaching has to explore the assessment of learning. Twenty years ago, a previous book by the same author and publisher, *The Teacher's Gradebook* (Raebeck 2002), dealt primarily with assessment. In this chapter we are discussing several comparable issues, with twenty years of additional experience and perhaps a bit of wisdom too.

Grades are the currency in most public secondary schools. Teachers are responsible for producing grades on a regular basis. Yet, in many schools there is little serious discussion of assessment practices and attitudes. Much or all of this is left to individual teachers. There may be wide disparity of methods and philosophy within the same academic department.

This essential function should be done in a thoughtful way. It also must be clear to students and parents the skills and knowledge being assessed and how this promotes learning. Students, already at the mercy of teachers' methods and personalities, need not be guessing, stressing, or legitimately complaining about how they are graded.

And as with being an educator in general, one's practices should be geared toward the higher good. Recall that learning itself happens in a context of What? How? Why? and To what end? A noble goal adds value to the experience. We are not simply punching kids' tickets for access to the next level. We are raising up educated, thoughtful, caring citizens for a world in need of such.

A highly effective teacher offers quality experiences of clear educational and social value. Accurately assessing student production and performance during these experiences is fundamental. Here—as with other key aspects of professionalism—reflection, modification, and innovation are key.

Let's begin with several tenets of successful assessment. Sound grading practices are:

- clear
- consistent
- fair
- flexible
- challenging
- appropriate
- transparent
- varied
- creative
- designed to promote learning

This means that students understand the criteria they are being evaluated on, as well as the evaluation process itself. They feel it is basically fair. Assessments can be quite challenging as long as the goals are attainable with effort over time. The teacher continually explains all elements of the grading process. And the teacher also revises and improves processes in order to keep them as effective as possible.

Schools and school systems are more or less flexible. Some may be overly rigid, requiring teachers to conform to mindless uniformity of curriculum and methods. Yet, in virtually all settings there remains a degree of autonomy for a tenured teacher. No one can legislate attitude. We are still responsible for the classroom gestalt, the vibe, the essential tone, and energy level. Along with this responsibility, an individual retains some control over his or her courses, and often quite a lot. The teacher determines much or all of the grading process, for instance. An effective teacher designs an effective process. An admirable teacher offers creative assessments that promote genuine learning.

Some generalities and themes to be aware of regarding assessment and grading follow:

GRADES
There is overgrading and overtesting in many classrooms.
US secondary schools test and grade students much more than colleges do.

Making it hard to fail is *not* the same as making it easy to get an A.
There is documented grade inflation in US secondary
 schools (Sanchez and Moore 2022).
100 is perfection and rarely attained in anything.
Giving lots of students 100 does not promote learning.
Giving lots of students 100 does not promote genuine self-esteem.
Success breeds success, and this can happen in small steps.
An A, a grade of 90, is a *good* grade.
Zeros destroy averages. Insist on students redoing unsatisfactory work.
It is unnecessary to grade every assignment.
Weighting assignments is a logical practice.
Grades should be seen as a by-product rather than an end-product.

STUDENTS
 Virtually all students can succeed academically.
 No one really wants to fail.
 Low achievers will stop playing a game if they don't believe they can win.
 Low achievers are often perfectly intelligent.
 There may be an undiagnosed underlying component
  to poor academic performance.
 Students should feel that the grading policies are "fair."
 Many kids care a great deal about their grades, even some who don't seem to.
 Students are impacted psychologically by their GPA
  and place in the academic hierarchy.
 Grades are arguably the largest source of stress in the academic realm of school.
 Self-esteem comes from genuine accomplishment.
 Students generally rise to the challenge.
 Students work harder for teachers they like.
 Students may also work harder on assignments they enjoy and see the value of.
 Students should be competing against their own potential, not with other kids.

PARENTS
 Parents want their children to be challenged and
  intellectually stimulated in school.
 Parents deserve to know the grading philosophy of the teacher.
 Open and professional communication with parents is essential.
 Parents want to feel that the teacher is fairly grading their child.
 The great majority of parents are supportive of
  appropriate grading practices, even if that

means somewhat lower grades.
Most parents value a challenging teacher.
Most parents see little educational value for their children from an "easy" grader.
Parents know that teachers wield power when it comes to grading.
Less educated parents may feel at a disadvantage with a teacher. Put them at ease.

TEACHERS
Remember that your class is one of many your students have each day.
Remember that your class is *not* the most important thing in any kid's life.
Effective teachers have effective grading practices.
Teachers' grading practices are congruent with their educational philosophy or lack of same.
Less effective teachers rely on conventional assessments.
More effective teachers develop unique and engaging assessments.
Better grading policies are clear and regularly explained. No mystery.
Ameliorate parent and student anxiety about your grading approach.
Grades should be a source of accomplishment for students, never punishment.
The goal is the learning, not the recording of the grade.
Effective teachers are flexible and offer multiple opportunities for success.
Maintaining standards means reasonable consequences for unacceptable performance.
Move students to caring as much or more about their production as the grade received.

OVERDOING IT

In too many public secondary schools students are subjected to an endless stream of grades, quizzes, tests, and other assignments. It is perhaps more surprising when they are managing all of this than when they become overwhelmed. Missing a couple of days can be disastrous. As previously noted, the typical American secondary school is chaotic, cluttered, disconnected, and antithetical to long-accepted learning theory and brain research.

If we set out to design a wonderful teaching/learning environment for adolescents and their teachers, it is doubtful that our best scholars and educators would arrive at a school of seven to ten periods of forty to forty-five minutes each with four minutes in between, with six to twelve mostly mandatory subjects per year, a different teacher for every one of them, constant, even daily, assessments, incessant fire drills, loudspeaker blather, mindless assemblies, mediocre food, cramped bathrooms, burdensome backpacks, and all of this mess beginning at 7:20–8:15 AM for 180 days more or less per year. Thus, we have tired, hungry, stressed-out kids who barely have time to pee. It is sadly absurd that so many school systems remain mired in this unproductive model (Steiner et al. 2022). Yes, adolescents are still young and much of what we do is mere babysitting. Some babysitters are better than others.

US colleges are considered the best in the world, yet their learning mode is entirely different from that of high school. (Might college enrollment increase if more kids knew how different and better it generally is than high school?)

Colleges have four to five courses per semester, perhaps one to three classes in any given day, wide-ranging course choice for students, most classes starting at 9 AM or much later, periods of fifty to one hundred and eighty minutes, at least ten minutes (and even several hours) between classes, and far fewer assessments. They also don't have loudspeaker announcements, incessant fire drills, or meaningless mandatory assemblies—and they are in session approximately 150 days per year. Perhaps colleges know that the high school model would be impossible to sell. It is ironic that our colleges are generally lauded and our high schools summarily criticized, yet we do little to make the high school academic experience more like that of college.

So don't overdo it! In a ten-week quarter offer two to three major assignments, two to three medium assignments, two to three minor assignments, and two to three ungraded or one-point assignments. (For weighting of same, please see the following text.) Eight to twelve grades/assessments in a quarter are plenty, yes? The first way to scale back is to give far fewer quizzes and tests. Other teachers are likely giving so many that students surely don't need more test-taking practice in your class.

Science teachers routinely grade labs unnecessarily. This creates busy work for them and stress for kids, always trying to make up labs which are too frequent and also may carry too much weight. Don't most students perform at a fairly consistent level? Aren't ten grades of 8/10 mathematically identical to one grade of 80/100? Why not give one grade per five weeks or per quarter that encompasses all lab work, keeping track of who is completing labs and their general quality simply by checkmarks and observation?

Friday can be a doomsday for students, with multiple tests and assignments all due at once. Why do we do this? Most likely it is done for teacher convenience and because it's conventional practice. Ask students when they would like an assignment to be due, and you may find that Tuesday is a favorite day. What do you lose in collecting papers on Tuesday instead of Friday? What is lost in allowing for student input in their learning experience? What is gained?

There is another proverb of Chuang Tzu's. It is known as "Three in the Morning":

> A monkey trainer went to his monkeys and told them:
> "As regards your chestnuts, you are going to have three measures in the morning and four in the afternoon."
> At this they all became angry. So he said: "All right, in that case I will give you four in the morning and three in the afternoon." This time they were satisfied.
> The two arrangements were the same in that the number of chestnuts did not change. But in one case the animals were displeased, and in the other they were satisfied. The keeper had been willing to change his personal arrangement in order to meet objective conditions. He lost nothing by it! (Merton 2004)

Use your old copies of multiple-choice quizzes and tests as "non-quiz quizzes." Let students pair up and go through it as a review of subject matter or recent reading, but don't give them a grade.

For an English teacher (and others), more than some multiple-choice test, a typed paper enables students to demonstrate knowledge and improve their writing ability. It also can be assigned seven to ten days before being due. This again offers students more control over their learning.

Though we don't want to overdo it, some teachers don't assign *enough* meaningful work. Ineffective teachers have too much downtime and not enough happening in their classrooms. Kids laxly looking at their cell phones with five minutes left in the period is not a pretty picture.

WEIGHTING ASSIGNMENTS

Show the class how weighting works. Let them know the mathematical difference in your varying numbers. Your method must be explained clearly and often. The heads of lots of kids (and adults) swim when dealing with more than a few even rudimentary numbers. So, be patient and stalwart while reading through this section on weighting. It is not as complicated as it may initially appear to be.

One source of confusion is that many kids (and adults) don't really understand percentages. When students (especially high-achieving ones) fail to do, or make up, a checkmark assignment and see a 0 in the computer, a sense of panic ensues. They mistakenly believe that 0 points out of a possible 1 has identical, rather than far less, impact as 0 points out of a possible 100.

If we accept that eight to twelve assignments per quarter is surely adequate, then we vary their importance and weigh them accordingly. Let's give major assignments 100 possible points. Let's give medium assignments 20–50 possible points. Let's give minor assignments 5–10 points and give 2 possible points for checkmark assignments. This last means simply recording that the work was completed with a check, and then translating that to 0 (if not done), 1 (if done adequately) or 2 (if done well) points the computer will register as a grade. And don't forget that you can do many valuable things with no grade or checkmark even.

So, if we have three major assignments worth 100 points each, that is 300 possible points. We have two medium assignments worth 50 points each, or 100 possible points. Then we have a 20 pointer and two 10 pointers, for another 40 possible points. Lastly, there are two 2-point checkmark assignments, such as a simple homework task or annotation of a short poem. That is 4 more possible points.

Let's add them up: 300 + 100 + 40 + 4 = 444 possible points this quarter.

Share these figures visually and on an accompanying handout. Then do some standard arithmetic to illustrate how weighting works. For instance, a hypothetical student gets 80/100 on each of the major assignments, 43/50 on each medium assignments, a 19/20, two 8/10's, and two 0/2's for not doing the checkmark assignments. This totals 361/444, or 81.3.

Using the same figures, but scoring 90/100 on the three major assignments, totals 391/444, or 88.1. Using the same figures from the previous paragraph, but adding 2 points for completing one of the checkmark assignments, totals 363/444, or 81.8.

In these examples students will see that doing better on major assignments impacts their grades far more. Some may even realize they needn't fuss about a point or two out of a possible 444. Yet, offering 2 points instead of 1 on the least weighted tasks will motivate some students to go for that single extra point and produce significantly better work.

Be sure to share the document detailing your weighting method and how quarterly and final grades are arrived at. Patiently answer any questions from students or parents. A sensible transparent grading system will do much to modify confusion and stress over the course of the year. (See *Gradebook Page* in appendix.)

CHANGING GRADES

Even with rational processes and thoughtful explanations there will be issues. No matter how conscientious, a teacher assessing thousands of items and recording thousands of grades will make mistakes. Students will come to you and say that they are the victim of such. This is no time to be defensive. Realize that students, especially the more ambitious, care a great deal about their grades. It means more to them than it does to you, or at least it ought to. Adolescents are particularly concerned with issues of fairness as well. Err on the side of leniency. Admit that it is possible you made a mistake.

Change the grade to the one the student believes is accurate. Leave it at that. No worries. Rather than lose student respect, you will gain admiration. Are 2 points (out of perhaps 2,000 possible in the term) a big deal? Give your students the benefit of the doubt. Put yourself in their place. Acknowledge the complexity of their daily experience. Look for patterns. Is this the only time this kid has asked for two more points? Or is it starting to look like grade grubbing? Even then, is it worth arguing about? Probably not.

Take the same approach with late papers or other assignments. Yes, it may be helpful to have a penalty of 5–10 points. Be careful in applying that, however. Again, look for patterns. Maybe this kid's excuse is completely legit. After all, she's never turned anything in late before. Just accept the paper and slip it into the pile, with a nod and a wink. Don't sweat it until the lateness becomes habitual. Then a lesson in responsibility and punctuality may be in order. Perhaps a lesson in kindness is equally welcome.

RUBRICS

Grading lots of anything is tedious. Reading, editing, and grading English papers, and then writing comments, is surely the most tedious part of being an effective English teacher. One component of being an ineffective English teacher is *not* regularly assigning, reading, editing, grading, and providing feedback, on student papers.

Social studies and science teachers should also assign papers and carefully review them several times a year. But English teachers are simply not teaching their subject if they are not assigning one and multi-page typed papers on a regular basis (at minimum three such assignments per quarter). Using rubrics can be a vital component in managing the substantial paper load that results while promoting better writing. Thus, developing clear, thoughtful, and accurate rubrics is essential. (More on rubrics in the following chapter.)

REDOS AND MAKEUP DAYS

We have noted that making it hard to fail is *not* the same as making it easy to get an A. Low achievers have low expectations. They may be perfectly willing to take a zero rather than complete a challenging task they don't feel confident about. Zeros kill grades. They should not be a grade option, or at most they should only be a last resort.

Instead, develop in the rubrics used for the assignment a threshold of performance. Any work not meeting the threshold has to be redone. It gets an "R" (for Redo) in your gradebook and incurs a 5- to 10-point penalty perhaps, but no full grade yet. Your threshold cannot be so low that a grade just above it threatens failure for the quarter. Neither can it be so high that there is little incentive to redo the work. A threshold of 60 is about right.

Ask the student to resubmit the assignment within a reasonable time frame and keep an eye on its completion. You will have to chase kids to do their make-up work, even stronger students at times. A strategy to accomplish this is to build into your schedule a "down day" every five weeks or so. Let them know about a week in advance that this is coming. Have something enjoyable planned as a reward for students who have all their work up to date. Then have the slackers make up their work wherever it is appropriate to do so. That may be your classroom, a study hall or test space, or the library.

A film or music video kids want to see can be an incentive. An ice cream party or the equivalent works. And a chess day is terrific. Offering adolescents the opportunity to play chess in a quiet and pleasant setting may prove unexpectedly popular. You do need rudimentary knowledge of the game and plastic chess sets, which cost about $20 each. As chess is a thinking game, administrators should see the value of doing that occasionally, especially if you are enabling other kids to make up work. Tell students that if they learn chess others will think that they are smarter than they actually may be!

When the Redos come in, grade them as if they are being received for the first time. Then affix a small penalty as a consequence of shoddy work. Instead of a zero, the student might receive a grade as high as a 90, or perhaps an 85 or an 80. Even a 70 is much better than a zero. And best of all, you got the kid to do the work!

GRADE INFLATION

It is tempting for each generation to assume that the following one has it easier, or is somehow less capable, disciplined, or ethical. In reality, people are not all that different by generation and adults have eternally moaned about the pathetic behavior of children (Socrates et al. 500 BCE and ever since).

There is anecdotal and even documented evidence of recent grade inflation, however. According to college admissions expert Jeffrey Selingo, citing College Board statistics, "About half of American teenagers now graduate high school with an A average, compared with fewer than 40% in 1998" (Selingo 2020). An A, once considered a good grade, is now seen as a minimum by many students and parents. Much of this has been fostered by lax grading standards and the proliferation of easy 100's.

You may note that in many secondary schools there is a clear disparity in grading. In the "core four" required courses of English, social studies, mathematics, and science (especially at the AP or honors levels) the grades are somewhat lower. In the elective areas, including foreign language, art, choral and instrumental music, and technology, grades are noticeably higher. We often see 100's across the board. Health and physical education classes, though required of all students, also offer 100's like gummy bears in many schools.

Then "harder" core class grades are simply combined with the "softer" elective grades into an overall GPA. One may find that a student has a big gap between the core and elective grades, with electives inflating the GPA decidedly. An overall GPA of 95 may actually be 90 in core classes. Of course, when high schools weight honors and AP classes (a most questionable practice) that stimulates further grade inflation.

A valedictorian who might have had a 96 GPA twenty years ago, now has a 103. A mediocre and well-meaning student who might have had an 86 twenty years ago, now has a 92. This would be fine if it meant superior performance and greater learning. But does it?

THE NATIONAL HONOR SOCIETY

The National Honor Society ostensibly requires superior achievement in its four pillars of service, leadership, character, and scholarship. School committees establish criteria based on that set by the national body, develop an application process, ask for eligible students to apply, determine who is admitted, and then monitor membership. Although the actual criteria for membership are largely determined locally, the National Honor Society is designed to be an organization comprised of the outstanding students in your school. Yet in some schools NHS is now little more than a social club.

In such, they are all too often comprised of honor roll students, with the honor roll (based on inflated grades) being as low as an 88–90 average. The pillars of service, leadership, and character may be equally wobbly. If it is to be an "honor" society, membership ought to mean something. It should be composed of excellent students, strong leaders, dedicated public servants, and young persons of impeccable character. That cannot be an overly large percentage in most high schools.

Oh, here come the shouts of elitism and exclusion. But is this tee-ball, where every six-year-old gets a trophy for showing up? These are sixteen- and seventeen-year-olds. Is there not clear selectivity and hierarchy in other elements of school and society? There is one starting quarterback, one first violin, one female and one male lead in the musical, one valedictorian, and one or two class presidents. That is not exclusivity, it is a competitive process. Everyone has a chance, and everyone has the right to fair competition. But no one is *entitled* to the pinnacle.

Some suggestions: In order to be eligible, students should be superior in at least three of the four pillars. *Scholarship* means a GPA of 95 and no grade below 80. *Leadership* means student government, a captaincy, club founder or officer, and Sunday school teacher. *Service* includes being a mentor to other students, helping regularly in the community soup kitchen, joining the junior fire department or EMT squad. And *character* requires student, faculty, staff, and administrative affirmation, an exemplary behavior record, strong attendance, and fine supportive conduct in school and out.

Such standards will both shrink numbers and elevate status. It will actually be an *honor* to be chosen and to serve. And if a student messes up, fails a class, is suspended from school, they're out. Standards are not optional in this case.

If you don't think your honor society should have such high standards for both acceptance and ongoing membership, that's fine. Don't have an honor society chapter. Call it the Anything Goes Easy Grades Club.

Chapter 9

More Terrific Assignments

The Book Non-Report or *BNR* assignment was introduced in Chapter 1 and will be expounded upon now. An extensive process, clear expectations, proper time frame, student choice, teacher oversight, exemplars, and an assessment rubric are key to making this experience valuable.

Quality literature is chosen by the students and teacher approved. The appropriate time is provided for the reading and resultant task, perhaps three weeks. Knowing that most students put off assignments as long as possible, we want to provide adequate, but not needless, time. Along with exemplars, the excellent past projects displayed in the classroom, a rubric is provided.

The rubric details teacher expectations while facilitating the grading process. As most of the projects will have little written work attached, they can be graded with a quick teacher observation and prompt completion of the rubric and grade. Checking a box is much faster than writing a comment saying the same thing. Providing clear and extensive teacher feedback, even for a complex and time-consuming student product, becomes much easier.

The longer writing pieces will be read carefully, yet that need not take too long to assess. Only a minority of students will choose to write an essay, a biography, a diary/journal, or an alternative ending. Again, the rubric is a fine aid here. It enables you to grade the class projects and return many rubrics in a day or two, with none taking longer than a week. Fast feedback is wonderful as long as it is thorough and accurate.

On the following pages are the assignment and rubric for *The Book Non-Report*:

THE BOOK NON-REPORT: TASK

You may choose any project from the following list. If you have a different idea entirely, please see me about that. Regardless of what you choose, your project will be graded based on the following:

- Creativity of the Idea
- Quality of Artistic Appearance
- Depiction of Two or More Literary Elements and/or Devices (NOT Including Plot)
- Attention to the Chosen Task
- Mechanics of Writing and Lettering
- Quality, Length and Rigor of the Novel Read

Choices

1. Book jacket or bookmark: Illustrate a cover for the book or design a bookmark with characters and/or the setting from the book.
2. Ending rewrite: Give the book a new ending.
3. Advertisement: Dress and act as a character from the book and "sell" the book to the class.
4. Character journal: Write a journal portraying a character from the book. The journal should be written in the first person and describe the character's thoughts, feelings, and ideas.
5. Poetry: Summarize the book by retelling the story in poetry form.
6. Map: Draw a map of the story setting to show story action. Use the map as a prop when discussing the book in front of the class.
7. Comic book: Summarize the book in the form of a comic book.
8. Illustrations: Draw or paint the main characters, setting, or climactic scene from the book.
9. Timeline/Story Board: Draw a timeline of events as they happened in the story or create illustrations as an outline of the sequence of major events.
10. News Report: Summarize the book by writing a news report as if the events in the story actually took place. Pretend to be a TV anchorperson and give the report to the class.
11. Three-dimensional project, sculpture, diorama, and so on depicting a climactic scene, including appropriate characters and setting.

Project Due: _____

THE BOOK NON-REPORT: RUBRIC

Rubric

Student_____ Score/Grade_____

3 = Excellently Fulfilled   2 = Capably Fulfilled   1 = Partially Fulfilled

	3	2.5	2	1.5	1
Creativity and Expression of the Idea					
Quality of Artistic Appearance and Lettering (if mainly art) and/or					
Mechanics of Writing (if mainly written): Paragraphing, Punctuation, CFC, Spelling, Usage, Syntax, Consistent Tense, Consistent Person and Point of View, Capitalization, etc.) ×2					
Full Depiction of Two or More Literary Elements—NOT including Plot—(Setting, Characterization, Theme, Conflict, Point of View) and/or Devices (Symbolism, Irony, Mood, Imagery, Tone, etc.)					
Attention to the Chosen Task and Overall Effort					
Quality, Length, and Rigor of the Novel Read					

Scoring/Grading   TOTAL: _____

18 = 100   17 = 96   16 = 92   15 = 88   14 = 84   13 = 80   12 = 76   11 = 72   10 = 68   9 = 64   8 = 60   Below 8 = Redo ®

Within the *BNR* rubric are the following components and themes:

- Proper Degree of Complexity
- Clarity/Expectations/Emphases
- Fairness and Transparency
- Stimulation of Learning
- Fostering Student Ownership
- Streamlined Grading
- Replaces Lengthy Teacher Comments
- Accurate Feedback
- Student- and Parent-Friendly Assessment

There are five criteria for assessment, and all but one (four) are worth three maximum points, or twelve total. *Quality of Artistic Appearance and Lettering/Mechanics of Writing* has double weight or six possible points. Combined that makes eighteen possible points. A full eighteen equates to a grade of 100. And there is a minimum grade of 60. Anything below that must be revised and resubmitted. Not doing the paper is simply not an option. Minimum grades help alleviate failure.

Notice how the rubric reflects and denotes what the teacher wishes to emphasize in the project. This is detailed to the point of listing major aspects of proper mechanics that are emphasized throughout the school year (CFC = commas for clarity), as well as giving mechanics, lettering, and artistic appearance double weight. At the same time *Creativity of Expression, Full Depiction of Literary Elements, Attention to the Chosen Task and Overall Effort,* and *Quality Length and Rigor of the Novel Read* all have strong places. The goal is quality.

Another terrific assignment (updated since *The Teacher's Gradebook*) is the *Autobiography Unit* done in the last quarter near the end of the term. This culminates with each student submitting a four- to six-page typed autobiography. It is best done toward the end of the school year because by then the effective teacher will have as much trust from students as may be gained. This way, students will be more likely to share things of importance. Often students will write more than required. This assignment also gives students lots of freedom of thought and expression.

The unit begins with several readings and activities designed to encourage students to reflect on what they value. Essays could include philosophical ones, such as Emerson's *Self-Reliance*, books by writers such as Malcolm Gladwell, Robert Reich, Steven Levitt, and Stephen Dubner (see bibliography) that explore complex social and psychological issues, current articles on societal trends, political trends and events, teen behavior, and any complex topics that are both educational and elicit student interest. Using songs, videos, podcasts, TED Talks, and poems is excellent in this unit. Discussing complex topics requires analysis and reflection and can lead to the formulation of informed opinions, rather than knee-jerk emotional reactions.

Following two or three weeks of such exploration the teacher can lead an activity designed to assist students in determining what they believe to be valuable in their own lives. We are not talking about any specific social, political, or religious view, of course. We are working toward development of thoughtful engaged young citizens attempting to make sense of the worlds they inhabit.

Upon assigning the autobiography itself, the teacher shares a document and rubric such as the ones following.

YOUR AUTOBIOGRAPHY: TASK

Your autobiography is about you: what you value, experiences that have shaped you, people in your life who have meant the most, dreams and aspirations, accomplishments, challenges, obstacles and adversities, hobbies, interests and passions, and anything and everything that makes you *you*.

Your topic may be fairly simple and certainly does not have to be earth-shattering. Some of us have had experiences that are more intense at this point, others maybe less so.

Just write about what you want to write about. This is an opportunity to reflect on where you are at this time of life, what you have noted from that, and where you may wish to go.

(If you are unsure what to write about, please see me and we'll talk.)

Regardless of what you choose to write about, your paper will be graded based on the following:

- Interest and Creativity of the Writing
- Attempt to Connect with the Audience
- Quality of Artistic Appearance and Photographs (if you choose to add or decorate)
- Attention to the Chosen Task
- Mechanics of Writing (Capitalization, Punctuation, CFC, Usage, Syntax, Consistent Tense, Consistent Person and Point of View, Paragraphing, Spelling, etc.)

And, yes, you will be writing in first person.

Due: _____

THE AUTOBIOGRAPHY: RUBRIC

Rubric

Student _____   Score/Grade _____

3 = Excellently Fulfilled   2 = Capably Fulfilled   1 = Partially Fulfilled

	3	2.5	2	1.5	1
Creativity and Expression of the Idea					
Quality of Appearance and Lettering (and illustrations, if art or photos are used)					
Mechanics of Writing (Paragraphing, Punctuation, CFC, Spelling, Usage, Syntax, Consistent Tense, Consistent Person and Point of View, Capitalization, etc.) ×2					
Attention to the Chosen Task and Overall Effort					
Quality of the Writing in Terms of Vocabulary and Sophistication					

Scoring/Grading   TOTAL: _____

18 = 100   17 = 96   16 = 92   15 = 88   14 = 84   13 = 80   12 = 76   11 = 72   10 = 68   9 = 64   8 = 60   Below 8 = Redo ®

Sometimes teachers emphasize creativity at the expense of mechanics or vice versa. Herein we see a balanced approach that values both sophisticated and careful writing. When utilized in concert with a previously shared list of correction symbols for mechanics (see the *Code of Corrections* in appendix), providing clear and extensive feedback is easier.

Even with an effective rubric, assessing a class full, or even a grade full of autobiographies is still a monumental task for an engaged teacher. A sound rubric provides structure and clarifies expectations. It leads to better student outcomes.

With the *Autobiography*, more than any other paper received, it may sometimes be necessary to write an extensive comment in responsive support. Also, it is appropriate to inform students that their story is confidential—unless they share something that legally requires teacher disclosure to guidance and/or administration.

EXEMPLARY RESEARCH

Providing exemplars—excellent former student products—heightens interest and stimulates quality performance. This is true of physical projects, such as dioramas or storyboards done for the *BNR*. It is also true of written work.

It is laborious to make dozens of copies of a superior multipage research paper. There is no better way to share your expectations and parameters, however. Have a stack available (or create a link) and offer it to students if they want one. It will still be necessary to explain each stage of the ongoing research experience. But after you have done this enough for many of the kids, there will be those who don't quite get it for whatever reason. Maybe when you went over this, and thoroughly, they were absent, sleepy, or dreaming of their first kiss. Simply saying "Look at the template paper" will save lots of time and confusion during such a complicated and important process.

Going through all the stages of writing an engaging research paper or report is a fine intellectual involvement. First share why this is both academically and practically valuable. For any student even contemplating higher education, learning how to prepare a research paper is quite worthwhile. And it is another opportunity to teach them the difference between opinion and *informed* opinion. This is imperative in today's hyper-distorted information environment.

Have the students choose questions of personal interest. Ask them to seek knowledge of something worth knowing in science, health, psychology, medicine, history, biography, and so on. Help them shape the question's syntax so that they are asking something specific and relevant. As always, you reserve the right to make suggestions and even rejections of mundane, frivolous, or tepid topics.

The title of the paper will be the question they are posing, such as "When in an Adolescent's Life is Peer Pressure Most Impactful?" or "Does Being a Vegetarian Affect Climate Change?" or "What Are Some Reasons Russia Invaded Ukraine?" Class time will be granted for research on laptops and in the library. The librarian can help with sharing tools and methods of accurate research. Notes are compiled. The stages of research and parts of the resultant paper are introduced. And the exemplar paper is offered.

This is a unit that will take as long as three weeks to complete. Although many students will do much of the research and writing outside of class, lots has to be explained and cataloged moving forward. It is a fine use of class time, of course, as it is a fine course of study. It is especially valuable to use class time to ensure that the less productive students may be successful.

THE SHORT STORY UNIT

People love stories. Sharing wonderful stories with your students is one of the delights of being a teacher. They may be yours, certainly. And they may be the professional work of others. And they may be stories from your students. What we seek are stories that have pace, style, and meaning; demonstrate good telling (or writing); and offer diverse powerful perspectives. Ideally, sharing a series of stories in a short story unit will lead to students writing fine stories of their own. Coming up with a viable and diverse modern list is challenging. There are lots of classics to choose from, yet some of them are no longer appropriate for reasons of content, interest level, or style. Then there are lots of newer ones, yet some of these are simply not as compelling or well-written as the classics.

The best stories are the ones that students respond to. Make sure you provide opportunities during and after the unit for your kids to let you know which stories they like or don't like, and why. Keep your list fluid and updated. It really doesn't matter if *you* think a story (or a film, novel, poem, or music video) is great if your students don't respond to it. At the same time, they may also respond to some awful dreck—and the effective teacher is raising their standards. There is endless judgment in this.

Ideally, sharing excellent stories during a three-week unit will culminate with surprisingly good student efforts. Offering two exemplar papers from previous years will stimulate quality productivity. Many students will likely exceed the maximum page number required. That means another serious effort of reading, correcting, and grading a boatload of short stories.

Using a rubric, exemplars, and the *Code of Corrections* all make your task somewhat easier. There is no getting around it; however, effective humanities teachers assign, read, and assess lots of student writing. Seeing the effort, creativity, and ultimate improvement in your students' writing provides gratifying energy to press on.

An overview of the written short story expectations and rubric is discussed next.

Valuable assignments require student engagement and effort. They also require teacher preparation and authentic assessment. If students groan at your mention of more "work," you'll know that there is room for creative improvement in the requisite tasks. When students eagerly ask, "What is our next assignment?" you'll know that your assessments are hitting the mark.

SHORT STORY: TASK

Your task is to write your own short story, with an appropriate title.

- Think in terms of the literary elements: compelling *plot*, intriguing *character(s) setting*, *theme*, *conflict*, and a focused *point of view*; and various literary devices such as *symbolism*, *irony*, *mood*, *tone*, *foreshadowing*, *characterization*, *dramatic irony*, *imagery*, and *diction*.
- Use descriptive and imaginative writing.
- Write with the end in mind—map out the plot beforehand.
- Avoid melodrama, which is excessive drama, such as mass suicides, aliens taking over the local supermarket, or the apocalypse.
- (BTW: If a story is written in first person, the narrator cannot die. It is a literary convention.)

The story is to be three to four pages, typed, 12-point TNR font, and 1.5 spaced.

DUE: _____

SHORT STORY: RUBRIC

Student_____   Score/Grade_____

3 = Excellently Fulfilled   2 = Capably Fulfilled   1 = Partially Fulfilled

	3	2.5	2	1.5	1
Creative and Original Plot Structure					
Mechanics of Writing (Spelling, Punctuation, Syntax, Grammar, Usage, Mechanics of Dialogue, Consistent Tense, Consistent Person, CFC, Paragraphing, Capitalization, etc.) ×2					
Attention to the Task (Length, Title, Inclusion of Literary Elements and Devices)					
Descriptive and Imaginative Language					
Clear Point of View and Consistent Voice, Organization, Appearance					

Scoring/Grading   TOTAL: _____

18 = 100   17 = 96   16 = 92   15 = 88   14 = 84   13 = 80   12 = 76   11 = 72   10 = 68   9 = 64   8 = 60   Below 8 = Redo ®

Chapter 10

Making and Keeping Parents Happy

It is easier to be effective when relationships are healthy and productive. Teaching is challenging under the best of conditions. Supportive relations with parents will surely increase teacher job satisfaction and resultant performance. Turn a dynamic that may be inordinately stressful into one that is smoothly beneficial. A teacher who is competent and caring can also build successful relationships with parents. A potentially difficult issue evolves into one of mutual respect and collaboration.

Many teachers are also parents of adolescents at some time. The teacher-parent dichotomy is another false one. Teachers and parents are natural allies, not adversaries. Cultivate that awareness.

Communication is elemental in any positive relationship. Accepting that parents are also taxpayers, and thus paying one's salary is instructive. Think of them as your clients. Strive to make them happy.

Providing an affirming, stimulating, and highly educational environment for their children and those kids' younger siblings pays off. Parents talk to one another, they get information from their kids, some are likely teachers in your school and district. Over time you will build a reputation as a "good teacher." That in and of itself is going to minimize problems with parents.

EMAILS AND PHONE MESSAGES

Being responsive is huge. No parent of yours should have to wait long for a reply to an email or phone message. That means the same day, if at all possible. There is little that is more important than this. Think of yourself as a businessperson dealing with customers. Parents are taxpayers—as noted, they are directly paying your salary. When they wish to share information, ask a question, or raise a concern, it is our obligation to respond promptly and professionally.

Often simply responding right away will defuse a potentially challenging situation. But be careful about what you put in writing. An email or a text message may not be the best way to resolve an issue, and it may feel to the parent that there is resistance or reluctance on your end. There is also far more room for confusion. Thus, a phone conversation is usually better. And if you feel that there is still potential for misunderstanding or needless upset, ask the parent to come and see you as soon as possible. Face to face is harder in some respects, but if the issue feels larger and possibly problematic, try to resolve it in person.

This approach also gains you respect and trust over time. You want the reputation of being open-minded and approachable. Parents will be more willing to behave in a comparable way. And if the issue really is not a big deal, or resolves itself, the parent won't bother coming into school anyway.

It is also desirable that your administrator refer parents directly to you. Your principal, assistant principal, or superintendent should never discuss the issue with the parent unless you have already had the opportunity to. If that is happening, however, let the administrator know that you prefer to initially deal with parental concerns directly. Then, if either you, the parent, or both feel that the issue remains unresolved, your administrator can play a mediating role.

OPEN HOUSE

Open house is a great opportunity for you. Think of it as a public relations event. It is your night to share what you feel is most important. It is a unique chance to meet your clients in your teaching/learning space. It is likely also brief and rushed. Recognizing this, script the experience to be as productive and positive as you can make it.

At open house, have a sincere greeting on the board. Provide your email and your cell phone number. Meet the folks as they enter your classroom.

Recognize that they are nervous too for all kinds of reasons. Their children are in your hands, and hopefully in your care.

Share your philosophy. Spend those precious few minutes reaching out on a human level. Tell them how honored you are to share time with their children each day—and that you love working with young people. Distribute copies of *What You Can Expect of Your Teacher*.

Tell them why you chose teaching and continue to find it meaningful. Read an inspirational passage. Thank the parents for finding the time and energy to come out at night to meet you. Ensure them that their offspring, the most important people in their lives, are well taken care of in your classroom.

Let parents know there is never any issue too small to discuss or any question too inconsequential to ask. Emphasize that you never wish there to be *any* confusion about a grade —and that they *must* contact you if there is. State that every student can be successful in your class.

Have copies of the syllabus for them and perhaps some other pertinent information but don't read through it. Don't be boring! Be engaging, appealing, and distinctive.

Tell a funny story. Note one or two wonderful experiences you have already had or intend to have with the students. Linger in the doorway afterward and be available for passing comments or questions. Don't rush away at the end of the night—stay and mingle in the lobby. Smile a lot!

PARENT CONFERENCES

At parent conferences have examples of current or recent assignments, assessments/rubrics, and the student's work. Explain your grading approach. Listen, listen, listen. You are working together toward student success.

Remind parents that you are always available, that kids may come after class or after school for help and encouragement. Let them know additional ways that students can improve their grades if that is an issue (see *Tips for Improving Grades* in appendix). Be willing to discuss the possibility of undiagnosed learning issues. Show that you are an advocate for them and their kids. Deliberately remove impediments.

As with open house, scheduled parent conferences can feel rushed. Be sure that you are fully able to deal with any issues of concern. If more time is required, schedule a follow-up meeting. A referral to guidance may be in order. Again, there is nothing more important than being of maximal assistance to parents.

With all of this being said, as with students, there are occasionally going to be truly difficult, confrontational, and even nasty parents. In any human population of any size there are extremes of behavior. That's not your fault. If you are professional, open, capable, and caring—known to be a "good teacher"—such experiences will be rare. Most likely, whatever you may have done to trigger a negative response is subsumed by that person's predisposition to seek conflict. No matter. You are now a target. You have to deal with it.

An appropriate emotional stance is "going soft." Initially do nothing. Say nothing. Just listen, as difficult as that may be. Take a few notes or pretend to. It is smart to allow someone who is upset to vent. Do not get defensive or emotional yourself. Again, this is difficult, even unpleasant, but essential. When you present as non-adversarial, it often will surprise the parent expecting a fight. That alone may defuse the situation.

When you do have an opportunity to speak, note that you have heard their concern. Perhaps restate it. Calmly say that you and the parent are on the same team: "We want the same thing for the young person in our care." Look for points of agreement. Find positive things to say about the student. Offer to make additional time if the meeting is going past its expected endpoint.

When it is appropriate, walk back through the process to see where the misunderstanding is. Be willing to admit a mistake or recording of an errant grade. Be intent on rectifying the perceived problem. Insist that conflict and confusion are the last things you want. Education of the student is paramount for you. Again, "We want the same thing for the young person in our care."

If you feel the situation is still volatile, see your principal as soon as you can and explain your side. Say what you have done and will do to resolve the problem. Ask for support. Then go home and have a stiff drink!

Chapter 11

Building Relationships

By this point it is clear that relationships are central to success as a teacher. "People first, program second." We have shared much about successful relationships with students. Then we noted the value of positive relationships with their parents. Let's finally focus on developing meaningful relationships with colleagues.

First, it is wise to consider every adult in your building, even in your district, a colleague. Yes, your teaching peers may occupy a prominent place. Likely some of your best friends will be in this group. At the same time, remember that although there is a hierarchy of salary and authority, we're all in this together. Treating the school secretaries cheerfully and respectfully may actually be as important to your effectiveness as doing so with the superintendent and school board members. Having a warm and courteous relationship with the custodian who cleans your room every afternoon will also make your job better—not to mention his or hers. Leave $20 in an envelope once or twice a year and notice immediate results. Call the cafeteria worker by her first name (most likely she is female). Ask for her to do the same with you. Smiling and joking may even get you an occasional discount!

These attitudes and behaviors may seem obvious. However, it is not simple or automatic to treat others with genuine warmth and consideration. We know that people are routinely less respectful of those they feel superior to. Teachers, often denigrated in our status-conscious society, may inwardly savor feeling superior to other people in the workplace. Resist that impulse. We are not identical to others, but we are all equal, yes?

As referenced earlier, the school day is hectic and stressful for kids. So it is for adults. We are dealing with hundreds of people of all types, ages, shapes, sizes, colors, personalities, and convictions on a continual basis. Finding moments in this madness to share the human experience with those we don't necessarily have to is yet another challenge. It is a welcome one when met with laughter, kindness, a listening ear, and a helping hand.

DEALING WITH THE BOSS

As noted, the first thing a teacher may forget is what it is like to be a student. And yes, the first thing some administrators forget is what it is like to be a teacher. Educators become administrators for a host of reasons. These include job advancement, salary increase, heightened authority, interest in new experience and challenge, teacher burnout or fatigue, ambition, idealism, and so on. Administrators may be deans, assistant principals, building principals, central office curriculum, budget, and personnel folks, or assistant and full superintendents. Many serve in a range of positions during their careers. Let's concern ourselves here with building principals and assistant principals, using the term "principal" for both.

Principals sometimes choose the role and other times find themselves in it. Regardless of why your principal is doing that job, it is helpful to recognize how difficult it is. Empathy goes a long way.

Be wary of saying, "I would/could never do that job" while judging everything the principal does. Routinely the principal is making decisions while having more information than a teacher has.

A teacher is generally concerned with the needs and concerns of teachers (especially one) and students, and secondarily with parents. A principal must be fully concerned with the needs of all teachers, students, guidance, support staff, and parents. While you may have direct responsibility for 100 to 150 kids, the principal has direct responsibility for all the kids, all the teachers, and all the other staff. Most teachers would *never* do that job.

Being a teacher can be lonely, but not as lonely as being a principal. The building principals have no peers. They are generally the only ones in their position. Being sincerely supportive and kind to your principal is not sucking up. Being respectful and open to suggestions is not being servile. Adopting helpful attitudes simply makes the school run better. Noting problems in a timely manner, and making concrete suggestions, can also be useful.

Maintain your integrity. Watch what you say publicly and privately. Don't undermine the leader casually or carelessly. Over time the principal will gain the reputation he or she has earned.

Additionally, find ways to let the leader know what you need from him or her. Find time for one-on-one meetings, and perhaps even go for a drink occasionally. Invite the boss to dinner. Connect on a human level.

Then when you ask for support in dealing with difficult parents or kids you're more likely to get it. Your principal will greatly value the friendship and respect of a dedicated teacher. Cultivate this trust.

OTHER TEACHERS

Of course, building relationships with support staff, guidance, and administration is demanding. Making time for your peers is difficult too.

A typical day consists of teachers and students rushing relentlessly from here to there. A snatched comment is far more likely than a conversation. Personal time is precious. There are always more things to do than time available to do them. We need to function as highly independent people in a highly interdependent system. This is not easy.

Put your colleagues first. Have an open door. Make sure you always have extra coffee or tea. Share materials and tasks. Tell others about a great book or film or song. Offer a not-too-off-color joke.

Assist peers with writing recommendations, choosing curriculum, or developing effective methods. Invite them into your room during a class and be willing to visit theirs. Counsel and advise about those tougher parents. Offer younger and newer teachers a shoulder to lean on and cry on, if necessary.

Know that even the strongest veteran teachers welcome support and camaraderie. Ask for their help, in part because people like to feel needed. Always reciprocate.

Yet here, as with other aspects of being effective noted in the preface, balance is vital. We have to shepherd our time and energy. Managing to do so while teaching in a secondary school is quite a skill. One need not be 100 percent available to others, and one need not neglect one's own duties. Being organized, modern, and present with your own students is the first charge, after all. Grading papers, developing fresh lessons, preparing materials, or just cleaning the coffee maker are all perfectly appropriate uses of your time in school. You may have to stay late or come early, however, if you don't want to take things home. That's just the way it is. It's called "work" after all.

Finding that balance of making your own systems hum while assisting others too is yet another challenge you will face. Embrace it. It isn't easy to be a good teacher, let alone a great one. It isn't easy to be highly effective in any profession, is it? Are there lots of great scientists, doctors, lawyers, managers, politicians, athletes, or carpenters? Why would anyone think it anything but supremely hard to be a great teacher? Being a good one, being effective, is a worthy goal.

As you build relationships and offer creative problem-solving your presence will be increasingly valued. Over time you will become known as a "go-to" person. Use the years and your experience to develop new tools, new energy, practical suggestions, and above all, resilience. Wisdom is a rare commodity.

Stay positive, even in trying hours or years. Beware of gossip and innuendo. Discourage students from ever talking negatively about another teacher in your presence. Of course, you know who the more or less effective teachers are—but it is not a competition. You also likely know where you stand.

Yet people can be competitive, jealous, and conniving. If you hear something disparaging or hurtful about you allegedly said by another teacher, most likely the best thing to do is nothing. Ignore it. But if it is a valid criticism, no matter the source, work to improve. Over the years, your reputation too will be well-earned. You can outlast the naysayers, those not getting the results and having as much fun as you are.

Find time to socialize outside of school. Again, everyone is busy. Domestic duties are constant. Yet socializing with peers is known to be one of the most emotionally satisfying and healthy things one can do (Shafir 2022). Make the time to at least occasionally go out together after work on a Friday. Seeing your colleagues in a different and more relaxed space can build relationships and workplace rapport. Those social experiences may include others from your building too, not just teachers. Invite administrators, secretaries, guidance counselors, custodians, whoever. Hierarchies rapidly dissolve in congenial social situations. Everyone may benefit.

Quality relationships are as sustaining as anything else in the secondary teaching experience. Walking into a building where you feel liked and supported is gratifying. Facilitate enjoyable human interactions while cultivating deep and lasting friendships. This provides endless rejuvenation in a grueling profession. Seek such and you will prosper. In time you may become the teacher you admired.

Chapter 12

Coda

Joyful Teaching

How is it possible to remain an enthusiastic, entertaining, engaged, and caring teacher for a week or a month, let alone a career? Is it even desirable?

Our work is intense. We deal with nearly every kind of student imaginable. All are expected to behave and learn. School boards may be wisely supportive, or they may be ignorant, meddling, overtly political bodies. Administrators may be competent and committed, or they may be decidedly less so. Parents may be respectful and understanding, or they may be raving about the latest social media–generated nonsense.

Teaching and public education are widely undervalued in much of America. Unlike many other wealthier democracies, funding of our schools remains grossly unequal, dependent far too much on property taxes designed to segregate by race and social strata.

> The U.S. educational system is one of the most unequal in the industrialized world. Students routinely receive unequal educational opportunities based on their social status. In contrast to Asian and European nations that fund schools centrally and equally, the wealthiest 10% of U.S. school districts spend ten times more per student than the poorest 10%, and spending ratios of 3 to 1 are common within states. Poor and minority students are concentrated in the least well-funded schools, most of which are located in central cities or rural areas, and funded at levels substantially below those of neighboring suburban districts. (Darling-Hammond 2001)

Professor Darling-Hammond wrote this twenty years ago, but of course it remains sadly so. Thus, classes may be too large, and spaces too crowded. Facilities range from modern and pleasant to crumbling and dismal. Quality materials are available unequally as well. Thus, school districts are struggling financially while teachers are grossly underpaid in many states and localities.

The current national average salary is about $65,000, ranging from lows of just $47,655 in Mississippi and $49,583 in Florida to highs of $86,315 in Massachusetts and $87,738 in New York (National Center for Education Statistics 2021). Of course, starting salaries are approximately half of the average, barely enough to live on in many cases. Pay is clearly a disincentive in such districts. It is surprising that there are any good teachers at all in some places. Those teachers are as much saints as they are educators.

With all of these challenges and a lack of compensatory financial incentives, what type of teachers might we expect to have on average? Well, average ones. Because there are so many valid reasons to remain average—while considering ourselves better than that, as we humans often do (Levitt and Dubner 2014).

It's been said that "you can't burn out if you were never on fire." And why risk burning out in the first place? It's smarter, perhaps, to do a decent job, care a fair amount, keep things conventional, and enjoy the weekends and holidays—if you don't have to work a second job!

Let's change the game a bit. Let's move to a more positive place. (You may have to physically move!) Assume that the job conditions are at least tolerable. We have a decent principal, an ethical superintendent, and a relatively hands-off school board. Classes are not crammed, and students are generally well-behaved. Colleagues are congenial and intelligent. Learning is taking place. Progress is being made. Though most kids don't love being in school, few actually hate it. The salary, though not great, is adequate in concert with a partner's.

Our wise friend Chuang Tzu said, "He who knows he has enough is rich" (Merton 2004). No one goes into teaching for the money. We just ought to have enough.

In such a scenario, there are far fewer reasons to simply be an average teacher. There are fewer excuses not to be good. Maybe it is possible to at least desire to be great.

Summon the motivation.

Excerpt from "Song of Myself," Walt Whitman, 1855, edited by Stephen Mitchell

Not I, not any one else can travel that road for you,
You must travel it for yourself.

It is not far . . . it is within reach,
Perhaps you have been on it since you were born,
and did not know,
Perhaps it is every where on water and on land.

Shoulder your duds, and I will mine, and let us
hasten forth;
Wonderful cities and free nations we shall fetch
as we go.

If you tire, give me both burdens, and rest the chuff
of your hand on my hip,
And in due time you shall repay the same service to me;
For after we start we never lie by again.

This day before dawn I ascended a hill and looked
at the crowded heaven,

And I said to my spirit, When we become the
enfolders of those orbs and the pleasure and
knowledge of every thing in them, shall we be
filled and satisfied then?

And my spirit said No, we level that lift to pass and
continue beyond.

You are also asking me questions, and I hear you:
I answer that I cannot answer . . . you must find
out for yourself.

Intrinsic meaning comes from knowing we are doing something valuable. Is there anything more valuable than educating the next generation? Developing sound young minds that are inquisitive, expansive, rigorous, and bold is surely as important as raising one's own children in a loving and creative way. Is there anything better than creating a haven of promise and compassion for a generation of aspiring young people?

Extrinsic rewards will include the admiration of students, the respect of peers, and the recognition of administrators. Parents will be increasingly supportive. Minor logistical problems will always be there, but psychological impediments will gradually diminish. Then each and every day holds promise and delight. Each class contains unexpected learning, unknown outcomes, and endless opportunity. Creativity flourishes. Joy predominates. Laughter is common. There is a palpable productive hum among your students. They love coming to your classroom every day. It may even be their highlight.

Yes, you are a joyful teacher. Despite the obstacles and your own human frailties, you are determined to thrive in the teachable moment.

You are that amazing teacher you admired when you were in school.

You are free-spirited, energetic, novel, witty, compassionate, and aware. You are clever, creative, thoughtful, respectful, challenging, and available. You are committed, modern, evolving, perceptive, and funny. You are spontaneous, inventive, eccentric, present, sensitive, flexible, and understanding. You are friendly, accessible, dedicated, well-dressed, professional, and in attendance every day. You are strangely delightful. You are hardworking, engaging, generous, courageous, and a role model for students yearning for direction.

Yet you manifest these attributes naturally, with love in your heart. It is not tedious, not a struggle going to work each day. Other than getting up so damned early, it's easy. You have learned that you are right where you should be—surrounded by vibrant human beings of various ages, shades, backgrounds, persuasions, and possibilities. You recognize that you have much to give, and continual blessings. You know that you are rich.

For you have chosen a wonderful profession. Beyond this, you have embraced a noble calling.

You are truly a good teacher. And you may even be a great one.

Appendix

WHAT YOU CAN EXPECT OF YOUR TEACHER

That I:

Am dedicated to teaching as well as I possibly can.

Believe that all students can be successful.

Respect the uniqueness of every student.

Am always willing to help the sincere student.

Contact parents when there is an issue that concerns them.

Work to assure that I am fair, consistent, and caring to all.

Listen to the point of view of students and parent/guardians.

Am professional in manner, speech, and appearance.

Maintain high standards of quality work and behavior for my students and for myself.

Enjoy what I do and try to make it enjoyable for my students.

Work cooperatively with other teachers and staff members, continually checking student progress and our effectiveness.

CODE OF CORRECTIONS

√	=	agreed, strong point
~	=	reverse order of words or letters
SP	=	spelling issue
/	=	insert a space
SYN	=	syntax issue
CFC	=	commas for clarity
WD	=	wrong word
—	=	cross out, omit repeated or weak word, such as "very"
X	=	start new paragraph
CAP	=	capitalize word
↓	=	move sentence/paragraph down
↑	=	move sentence/paragraph up
T	=	improper/inconsistent tense
POV	=	improper/inconsistent point of view
R	=	redo/rewrite paper
OK	=	okay, ignore teacher symbol erroneously placed

TIPS FOR IMPROVING GRADES

So, your grades are not what you (and your parents) wish they could be?

1) Redouble your efforts: hard work is essential to success
2) Do your homework routinely—put away the electronic devices!
3) Establish a study schedule and stick to it
4) READ, READ, READ, READ: always have an "outside" reading book
5) Ask the teacher(s) how you can get better grades
6) Make sure you are seated front and center in classroom
7) Act the part of a serious student in every class
8) Offer to do extra credit
9) Stay for extra help
10) Improve study strategies:
    a. highlight
    b. use color markers and code different topics, subjects, etc.
    c. take clearer, more extensive notes

    d. review more often
    e. get an older textbook that you can write in
    f. maintain healthy sleep patterns
    g. maintain healthy diet and lifestyle

11) Share papers with someone prior to handing them in, for editing help. Sometimes a teacher will offer that service too. Worth a try.

Remember: teachers give breaks to kids they like,
respect, and know are committed.
Be that kind of student, and your grades will quickly go up.

TIPS ON TAKING NOTES

- *Use the text style to identify important points:*
  Become familiar with the font, symbols, borders, graphics, colors, and layout that highlight main ideas or terms
  Be alert to the writer's goal: highlight ideas/references/opinions that seem significant
- *Taking notes while reading*
  Include headings, key terms, and graphics
  Take down only the important ideas: be brief but clear
  Summarize in your own words
  Use symbols to highlight for review
  Use textbook review questions to develop study questions
  Make copies of text so that you can annotate/highlight
- *Review textbook notes*
  Identify main ideas
  Fill in details for better understanding
  Identify unclear information and/or questions
  Delete unnecessary information
  Review note organization; add symbols and rewrite notes
  Write a summary
  Color code notes/sections/highlights with markers
- *Taking notes during a lecture*
  Listen actively—think before you write, and keep it brief

> Be open-minded. Don't let arguing affect your note taking
> Keep notes in a large notebook and use a clear format
> Listen for cues and key words
> If it's on the board . . . Write it down!
> Have a consistent system for taking notes

- *Why take notes?*
  > Good notes will stimulate critical thinking and engage you.
  > Note taking helps you remember what happens in class.
  > Good notes can make studying easier.

Use a note-taking system like Cornell Notes System that provides space for you to ask questions while you take notes and to summarize your notes each evening.

Note: make it a habit to see your teacher regularly outside of class and especially before a test or major assignment is due.

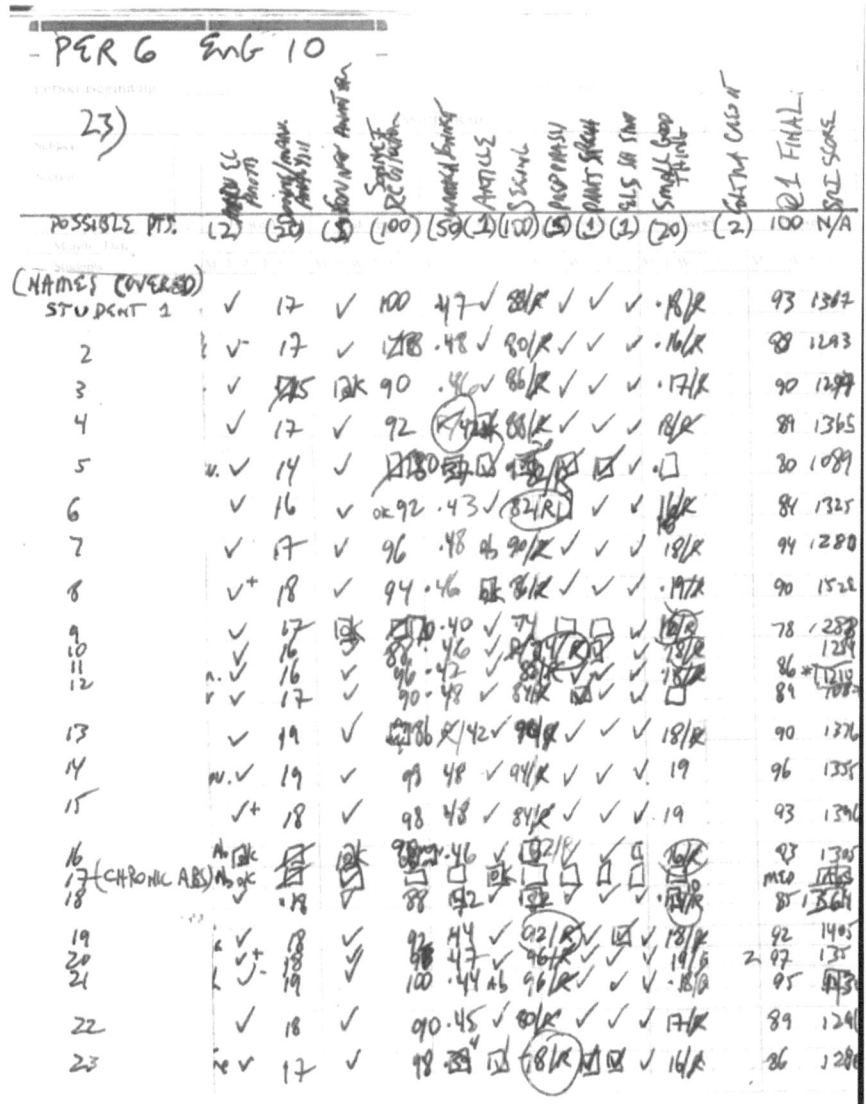

Figure A.1. Actual Page of Barry Raebeck's Gradebook for a Mixed-Level English 10 Class.

Bibliography

Bouchrika, I. 2022. *Teacher Burnout: Challenges in K-12 and Higher Education.* Research.com. https://research.com/education/teacher-burnout-challenges-in-k-12-and-higher-education.

Darling-Hammond, L. 2001. Inequality in Teaching and Learning: How Opportunity is Rationed to Students of Color in America, Chapter 9 in Institute of Medicine. *The Right Thing to Do, The Smart Thing to Do: Enhancing Diversity in the Health Professions – Summary of the Symposium on Diversity in Health Professions in Honor of Herbert W. Nickens, M.D.* Washington, DC: The National Academies Press. https://doi.org/10.17226/10186.

Ginott, H. 2022. *Congruent Communication Theory in Classrooms.* Study.com. https://study.com/ academy/lesson/ginotts-congruent-communication-theory-in-classrooms.html.

Gladwell, M. 2005. *Blink: The Power of Thinking Without Thinking.* New York: Little, Brown, and Company.

Gladwell, M. 2008. *Outliers: The Story of Success.* New York: Little, Brown, and Company.

Gladwell, M. 2014. *David and Goliath: Underdogs, Misfits, and the Art of Battling Giants.* New York: Little, Brown, and Company.

Glasser, W. 1985. *Control Theory in the Classroom.* New York: Harper and Row.

Jacobson, R. 2022. *Social Media and Self-doubt.* Child Mind Institute. https://childmind.org/article/ social-media-and-self-doubt/.

Jensen, F. and A. Ellis Nutt. 2015. *The Teenage Brain: A Neuroscientist's Guide to Raising Adolescents and Young Adults.* New York: Harper.

Levitt, S. and S. Dubner. 2005. *Freakonomics.* New York: Harper Collins.

Levitt, S. and S. Dubner. 2009. *SuperFreakonomics.* New York: Harper Collins.

Levitt, S. and S. Dubner. 2014. *Think Like a Freak*. New York: Harper Collins.

Merton, T. 2004. *The Way of Chuang Tzu*. Boston: Shambhala.

Mitchell, S., ed. 1998. *Song of Myself: Walt Whitman*. Boston: Shambhala.

National Center for Educational Statistics. 2021. *Average Salaries of Elementary and Secondary Teachers in the U.S.* https://nces.ed.gov/programs/digest/d21/tables/dt21_211.60.asp.

National Institute of Mental Health. 2020. *Suicide is a Leading Cause of Death in the United States*. Washington, DC: NIMH.

National University. May 13, 2021. *The Negative Effects of Technology on Children and What You Can Do*. https://www.nu.edu/blog/negative-effects-of-technology-on-children-what-can-you-do/.

Promoting Relationships and Eliminating Violence Network. 2022. *The Difference Between Teasing and Bullying*. Kingston: PREVNet Administrative Centre.

Raebeck, B. 1998. *Transforming Middle Schools: A Guide to Whole-School Change, 2nd Edition*. Lancaster, PA: Technomic.

Raebeck, B. 2002. *The Teacher's Gradebook: Strategies for Student Success*. Lanham, MD: Rowman & Littlefield.

Reich, R. 2018. *The Common Good*. New York: Alfred A. Knopf.

Sanchez, E. and R. Moore. 2022. *Grade Inflation Continues to Grow in the Past Decade*. ACT Research Report.

Selingo, J. 2020. *Who Gets In And Why: A Year Inside College Admissions*. New York: Scribner.

Shafir, Hailey. 2022. Social Self. https://socialself.com/blog/socialize-work/.

Steiner, E., et al. 2022. *Designing and Sustaining Innovative High Schools: Successes, Challenges, and Student Outcomes*. Santa Monica, CA: Rand Corporation. https://www.rand.org/pubs/research_briefs/RBA322-1.html.

Thoreau, H. D. 1854. *Walden: Or, Life in the Woods*. Princeton, NJ: Princeton University Press.

Whelan, R., ed. 1991. *Self-Reliance: The Wisdom of Ralph Waldo Emerson as Inspiration for Daily Living*. New York: Crown.

Zakaria, F. 2015. *In Defense of a Liberal Education*. New York: W.W. Norton.

Index

adolescent brains: still developing, 18
advanced placement (AP), 17, 22–23
affirmative action, 17
Anything Goes Easy Grades Club, 60
assessment: generalities and themes of, 50–52; promoting learning, 49; tenets of successful, 50
assignments: balance of, 53; distribution of, 55; late, 56; weighting, 54–56
Attention Getting Device (AGD), 45
autobiography rubric, 67
autobiography unit, 64–68

balance, of joy and rigor, 43
"Becoming Highly Literate" (slogan), 12
BNR assignment, 62
BNR rubric, 63
Book Non-Report (*BNR*), 2, 41, 61, 68

cell phones, student use of, 6–7
Chapter Masters, 7–9, 22
chess days, 57–58
Chuang Tzu, 84; "The Empty Boat," 33–34; "Three in the Morning," 54

classes: daily objectives for, 1–12; maintaining focus, 4–5; playfulness, 43; starting calmly, 34–35
classroom: additional touches for, 41–42; carpeting of, 42; comfortable seating, 40; equipment for, 40–42; as home, 39; library, 41; lighting of, 40; as Museum of International Culture, 41; music in, 40–41; quiet in, 42–43; silencing PA, 4, 45; as theater, 43
"Climb Ev'ry Mountain," 47
Code of Corrections, 68, 70, 88
college format, 53
collegial relationships: peers, 79–80; principal, 78–79; staff, 77
Common Core, 11
cooperative learning, 18–20
"Creating a Community of Scholars" (slogan), 13, 32, 38, 40

Darling-Hammond, Linda, 84
direct instruction, 8
disciplinary referral, as last resort, 36

Dominant Positives and Dominant Negatives (DPs and DNs), 35–37
down days, 57
Dubner, Stephen, 65
Dylan, Bob, 2

Gladwell, Malcolm, 65
Glasser, William: *Choice Theory*, 27; *Reality Therapy*, 27
the Golden Golf Club, 44
Gradebook Page, 56, 91
grades: changing of, 56; as currency, 49; inflation of, 58–59
group grade, problems with, 19
Gumby, 47

habits of mind, reinforcing good, 15

illusion of choice, 2
"I messages" (Ginott), 36
Individual Education Plan (IEP), 9, 37
Internal Field Trip, 46
interruptions, annoyance of, 4–5
iPads, 5

Jagger, Mick, 4

Le Chapeau de le Dunce, 45–46
Levitt, Steven, 65
Literary Elements and Devices (LEDs), 8

Mrs. Martinet, 4, 42
My Fair Lady, 47

National Center for Educational Statistics, teacher salaries, 84
National Honor Society, standards for, 59–60
National Institute of Mental Health, 28
non-quiz quizzes, 54

"Ode on a Grecian Urn" (Keats), 46
The Old Man and the Sea (Hemingway), 3
open house, 13, 45, 74–75
opinion *versus* informed opinion, 68

Pair/Share, "Turn To," 19
parents: challenging ones, 76; communicating with, 73–74; conferences, 75–76; sharing syllabus with, 75; supportive relationship with, 73
people first, 77
Power T, classroom seating, 37
pragmatic idealism, 37
Pride and Prejudice (Austen), 41

"Readers Are Leaders" (slogan), 12
redos, 57–58
Reich, Robert, 65
research: exemplary unit, 68–69; project, 19
response journals, 14–15
rubrics: to facilitate grading, 56; threshold of performance, 57; using, 8

see me after class (SMAC), xiv, 37
selective hearing, 33
Self-Reliance (Emerson), 5
short story rubric, 72
short story unit, 12, 69–71
SMART Board, 5, 7–8, 12
Socrates, 58
Socratic seminar, 21
"Song of Myself" (Whitman), 85
"Sonnet 18" (Shakespeare), 4

sonnet recitation, 8–9
The Sound of Music, 47
the Steel Rod, 45
students: buy-in, 11; caring about, 25–29; consequences rather than punishments for, 33; deeply troubled ones, 37–38; diverse groups of, 22–23; don't want to be in trouble, 35; expectations for, 18; fear of public speaking, 9; getting paid, 15–16; identifying with, 17; morale of, 32–33; pep talk to, 28–29; professional distance from, 25; reading picture books, 42; stepping outside with, 35–36; teasing of, 44; trust from, 27–28
student writing: grading selectively, 14; for its own sake, 15; motivation for, 15

The Teacher's Gradebook (Raebeck), 49
teachers: as actors, 43; artfulness of, 33; classroom reflects attitude of, 41; as counselors, 26–29; effective questioning, 20–22; gaining respect from students, 13; monitoring impact on students, 43; undervalued in the United States, 83–84; varied roles of, 29; writing recommendations, 29–30
teaching/learning, 17, 33, 52
teasing *versus* bullying, 44
technology, problems of, 6
TED Talks, 65
teen suicide, 27–28
Thoreau, Henry David, 13
Tips for Improving Grades, 75, 88–89
Tips for Taking Notes, 89–90

What You Can Expect of Your Teacher, 13, 75, 87
"Writers Are Brighter" (slogan), 12

YouTube, 40

zeros, as destroyers of grades, 57

About the Author

Barry Raebeck is a professional educator, author, and consultant with forty-five years of experience. Having received his BA in English with high honors from Wesleyan University, Barry earned his MS in reading and elementary education from Long Island University and his PhD summa cum laude in educational leadership from the University of Virginia. He has served as a teacher, counselor, coach, principal, headmaster, director of curriculum, interim superintendent, and consultant. He taught English at Southampton High School on Long Island for twenty-three years, working with a highly diverse group of students at all grades and levels.

Barry founded the college admissions consulting firm Your College in 2006. The focus remains on matching kids to colleges they are best suited for. He has enabled hundreds of high school students to be admitted to terrific schools.

Author of a dozen articles in the field of education and two prior education books, *Transforming Middle Schools: Guide to Whole-School Change* and *The Teacher's Gradebook: Strategies for Student Success*, Barry has presented over a hundred times on educational topics and has consulted with various school districts on essential aspects of school improvement.

He has also authored a novel, *Tyger on the Crooked Road: William Blake—Poet, Painter, Prophet*. As a result, he has lectured in England several times on Blake's inspirational life.

The father of three grown-up daughters and proud grandfather of four, he lives with his wife, Susan, in Wainscott, New York. Barry can be contacted at braebeck@optonline.net.

www.ingramcontent.com/pod-product-compliance
Lightning Source LLC
Chambersburg PA
CBHW021859230426
43671CB00006B/457